THE AUTHOR

PRINCIPLES AND PRACTICES OF PASTORAL CARE

Books by Russell L. Dicks

The Art of Ministering to the Sick
(Co-author with Richard C. Cabot, M.D.)

Pastoral Work and Personal Counseling

Who Is My Patient?

My Faith Looks Up

And Peace at the Last
(with Thomas S. Kepler)

Meet Joe Ross

Toward Health and Wholeness

How to Make Pastoral Calls for Ministers and Laymen

Principles and Practices of Pastoral Care

Premarital Guidance
(In preparation)

PRINCIPLES AND PRACTICES OF PASTORAL CARE

RUSSELL L. DICKS, B.D., D.D., Litt.D.

PRENTICE-HALL, INC., ENGLEWOOD CLIFFS, N.J.

Principles and Practices of Pastoral Care
by Russell L. Dicks, B.D., D.D., Litt.D.

Library of Congress Catalog Number: 63-8623

Printed in the United States of America

Prentice-Hall International, Inc.
(*London, Tokyo, Sydney, Paris*)
Prentice-Hall of Canada, Ltd.
Prentice-Hall de Mexico, S.A.

70192-T

To

Richard C. Cabot, M.D. and Anton T. Boisen, D.D.

Who, together, launched the clinical pastoral education movement for clergy.

INTRODUCTION

This series of books represents the most comprehensive publishing effort ever made in the field of pastoral care. These books could not have been published twenty-five years ago, or probably even ten, for the material was not then available. In the past, single books have been available covering different phases of the task. Now we are bringing the subjects together in a single series. Here we present a library of pastoral care covering the major topics and problems that most pastors will encounter in their ministry. Fortunately, not all of these problems need be faced every week or even every month. But, when they are, the minister wants help and he wants it immediately.

These books are prepared for the non-specialized minister serving the local church, where he is the most accessible professional person in the community. It is a well-accepted fact that more people turn to clergy when in trouble than to all other professional people. Therefore, the pastor must not fail them.

Russell L. Dicks

PREFACE

I stood at the edge of the world and asked, What of life?

What of love?

What of pain?

What of feeling?

Who lives, who loves, who hurts, who feels?

I asked, but I heard no answer;

Only the emptiness of waves upon the shores, of wind in the trees, of sunshine and growing things in the land, the sea and air.

I turned my face to the sky, the sea, the mountains, the open spaces,

To the big things of the world about me,

Nothing came back that I could understand.

I turned my face to the cities and farms, to factories and schools and places of learning,

A babble of many voices and many people came to me in many tongues and many noises,

Some said words without meaning and others made sounds without words.

I said, It is because I do not understand their language for all are talking. The fault is mine because I have not learned to understand,

And I was angry at my ignorance.

A child took my hand and smiled;

I put my arms around her and felt the warmth of her small vibrant body against mine;

In her I felt love and I was not alone.

I said, I will learn their language and then I can understand. I have time now for love, even the love of a small child gives me contentment and courage and meaning. Love gives me curiosity and patience and a tomorrow.

CONTENTS

PRINCIPLES AND PRACTICES OF PASTORAL CARE

PART ONE

PRINCIPLES

ONE

WHAT IS PASTORAL CARE?

Pastoral Care relates to people irrespective of their creed, social position or prestige. It is the concern shown for the needs of men in every walk of life; from the bricklayer to the structural engineer, from the Olympic star to the paraplegic, from the school girl to the grandmother. Whether in the prime of health or incurably ill, in joy or sadness, in good times or bad—there may be a need for pastoral care. The clue to the need is the recognition of the point where life's stress and strain affect body and soul. It deals with people but particularly it deals with people in trouble. Pastoral care is shared compassion.

It is as old as religion, as old as human existence we believe, going back far beyond the Judeo-Christian tradition to the primitive medicine man. Wherever one person turns to assist another there is pastoral care. It progresses through a tribal leader to a Moses, called of God, not only to lead his people but to heal their disputes as well; it is the early physician with his herbs, his simple surgery and his magic; it is the healer with his prayers, his incantations and his magic. Wherever and for whatever reason—pain or panic, sadness or joy, awe or adoration—one person turns to another to seek help or to proffer it, to share sorrow or to share strength—there is the impulse for pastoral care.

Pastoral care cannot be understood by the study only of its techniques. One must study also the people of pastoral care and the relationships between those people. Further, since pastoral care is carried on by pastors one must study religion as it functions in and through the persons in the relationship. Psychology studies the behavior of people, whereas religion provides the hope for these same people regardless of their behavior. Psychology focuses upon human relationships as they are while religion inspires and motivates people to change and improve their condition. Supported by psychology and religion the pastor moves into the arena of relationships and becomes an active participant. Pastoral care is involvement; involvement in the relationship. While it includes reflection on the part of parishioner and pastor both during the action and later, it is still essentially action.

The counselee has a problem. He turns to the counselor or the counselor seeks him out (for the action may be initiated from either side), and something new has been added—the relationship, the emotional-intellectual interplay between two people. The intensity of the relationship, its meaningfulness, strength, and contribution will depend upon the role it plays, which in turn depends upon the needs of the counselee for help and the skill of the counselor in helping. It is clear, therefore, that the counselor must know his own emotional stature before he can help others.

The New Pastoral Care

While pastoral care as a practice is as old as religion, it has made greater advance since 1925 than in all of its prior history. The term "pastoral care"[1] was first introduced in the ninth century when a book by that title, originally written in 590, was translated. The author, Bishop Gregory, had written it in protest to his elevation to the high office of Pope.

In 1925 Bishop Angus Dun, then a professor at the Episcopal Theological Seminary in Cambridge, Massachusetts, first suggested that we accept this term to describe our work in the early days of pastoral clinical education. It has gradually come into wide usage, together with the term "pastoral counseling," as the minister's work with individuals has picked up interest both among the laity and clergy.

I have always preferred the term "pastoral care" as the over-all term to describe the work with individuals to distinguish it from the ministry of preaching, teaching, church administration and music. Pastoral care can be further subdivided into: "pastoral calling" in

[1] *Pastoral Care*, translated by Henry Davis, S.J. (Westminster, Maryland, The Newman Press, 1950).

which the pastor goes to the people, and "pastoral counseling" in which the people come to the pastor. These will be discussed more fully in a later chapter.

As early as 1922, Richard C. Cabot, M.D. formerly professor of medicine at Harvard Medical School, wrote in the *Survey Graphic* suggesting a year of clinical training for theological students. Here he advocated that seminarians should have a year's supervised experience with people suffering from the "infirmities of mankind," just as medical students do before going to their work as licensed physicians. These infirmities would be found in general and mental hospitals, prisons, and in homes for the aged. In 1925 The Reverend Anton T. Boisen, a Congregational minister, following an emotional illness, became the first full-time Protestant chaplain in a state mental hospital in America. Dr. Boisen and Dr. Cabot together launched the plan by taking theological students into the Worcester State Hospital, Worcester, Massachusetts, for this experience. Amongst the early students were H. Flanders Dunbar, M.D. now deceased, A. Phillip Guiles, Ph.D. now deceased, who became the first professor of pastoral care to come out of the new clinical pastoral education effort. Dr. Guiles taught at Andover-Newton Theological Center, Newton Centre, Mass. Other early students were the Reverend Donald Beatty, now assistant to the director of the Veterans Administration Chaplaincy Service, Carroll Wise, Professor of Pastoral Care, Garrett Biblical Institute, Evanston, Ill., and Alexander Dodd now in private counseling.

Boisen, Cabot and Guiles and others laid the foundation for what was called at first "clinical pastoral training" and later "clinical pastoral education." Dr. Henry Pitney Van Dusen (Union Theological Seminary, New York) once said that it had influenced the Protestant church more than any other effort, except the founding of the World Council of Churches, since the Reformation. One wonders whether Dr. Van Dusen would not drop this lone exception if he were closely familiar with what clinical pastoral education has meant to the church in terms of salvaging marriages, strengthening home life, restoring health of mind and body to the tense and disturbed, and bringing courage, hope and dignity to those facing incurable illness and death.

The Council for Clinical Training, Inc. was incorporated in

1930 with Dr. Cabot as its first president and Dr. Guiles as its director. In 1935 Dr. Guiles launched his own independent work with the support of the Earhart Foundation and the first serious split within the fledgling movement had taken place, a clash that has continued in various forms until the present time.

In 1933, I went to the Massachusetts General Hospital as chaplain by appointment made possible by Dr. Cabot's prestige and with his financial support. At the end of the first summer, Dr. Cabot asked me to report on my program and progress. I showed him written notes of my work with selected patients. After reading them, Dr. Cabot said to Miss Ida M. Cannon, Chief of the Social Service Department, "This is the craziest thing I have ever seen. Here is a man who writes down the conversations and prayers he has with a dying patient. We had better ask him to stay on here awhile. We might learn something."

In 1936 Dr. Cabot and I collaborated in the publication of *The Art of Ministering to the Sick*[2] which became the spearhead book for clinical pastoral education. For the first time, a doctor and minister sat down to write together. Our thoughts were so interwoven in many chapters that when we had completed the manuscript we did not know where one had left off and the other began. Equally important were the verbatim conversations between patient and pastor that were included. The clinical reflective study method was now under way, and has since come to be widely used throughout clinical pastoral study.[3]

At that time, neither Dr. Cabot nor I knew much about grief, as it has since been described for the clergy. Dr. Cabot felt the pastor should be "the general" in managing the patient in "the wholeness" of his total need. While he understood the limitation of the physicians' understanding, I sensed the physicians' position better. I knew that no one could supersede the doctors' control of the patient. I was convinced that the pastor's role in the sick room should be supportive to the physicians'.

Dr. Cabot's experience in medicine preceded modern psychiatry.

[2] This volume has gone through twenty printings. A Swedish edition appeared in 1962.

[3] *Casebook in Pastoral Counseling,* edited by N. S. Cryer, Jr. and J. M. Vayhinger (Nashville, Abingdon Press, 1962).

He was impatient with psychiatry because it was too vague, too ethereal. Trained as he was in medicine and philosophy, he could be expected to express a strong belief in God as the Healer. He felt that psychiatry was neither scientific nor philosophical; so little reference to psychiatry was made in *The Art of Ministering to the Sick.* Dr. Cabot and Dr. Boisen differed over the idea that the healing force of God, which Dr. Cabot described so graphically in Chapter IX under the topic of "Vis Medicatrix Dei," also operates in the area of mental-emotional health. Boisen, of course, was right and one wonders how Cabot could have failed to see this. Probably it was because he had been so long involved with physical illness.

Dr. Boisen's illness[4] had been mental. His work was in the mental hospital with the mentally ill. He and his students naturally identified with psychiatry. My illness was physical[5] and my work was in the general hospital with people who suffered physically. My students and I identified with old line medicine; the old and well established specialties. Psychiatry was just beginning to make inroads into the general teaching hospitals. Its influence upon the general practitioner was remote. The first in-patient service for mentally ill was established at the Massachusetts General Hospital, third oldest hospital in the United States, while I served as chaplain there from 1933–1937.

Clinical pastoral education has followed these two main streams of thought. Each made its own contribution; each fought for its point of view, and frequently to the detriment of the other. In spite of these differences, steady and rapid progress was made in establishing chaplaincy services in institutions.

Today, over a thousand Protestant clergy serve as full-time general hospital chaplains, including V.A. hospitals. More than half of them are accredited by the American Protestant Hospital Association. Nearly all state mental hospitals have chaplains, almost all of whom have had specialized training. Impressive advances are evidenced in the prison chaplaincy, although not much literature is available on this ministry. Major theological seminaries now have professors of

[4] See *Exploration of the Inner World* and *Out of the Depths* (New York, Harper & Row, Publishers).

[5] See *Toward Health and Wholeness* (New York, The Macmillan Company, 1960) pages 96–98.

pastoral care who have come to their appointment from clinical pastoral experience, many of them with advanced degrees. Even more important than the above has been the steadily growing influence upon the work of the local pastor. Now he fights for time to do his work because the pastoral task is so heavy.

When we began our work at the Massachusetts General Hospital the sick room was practically closed to the pastor, particularly if the patient was seriously ill. Today, the minister is expected to call regularly. He is expected to minister with judgment and hope, much as the doctor is expected to perform with skill and knowledge. Our understanding of the art of helping people is advancing steadily, although it is far from complete, or even adequate, in many areas. The "*new pastoral care*" has many frontiers. Our immediate purpose here is to provide background information helpful to the understanding of our present situation. Later we shall discuss the specific areas of Pastoral Care in which the clergyman is involved.

The Growing Edge of the New Pastoral Care

The development of the new pastoral care, the unfolding of the task and its description has been a slow, steady and often tedious process. There were long and lonely days when we wondered what we were doing; there were exciting experiences that were encouraging; there was the slow accumulation of clinical data that backed up our emerging convictions. We started only with the recognition of need. Dr. Boisen had felt that religion contributed to his recovery from psychotic illness; yet he did not find a practitioner of religion (pastor) in the hospital with whom he could talk as he began to emerge from the loneliness of mental confusion. There was then no man of God with the theological insights and the depth of experience with mental anguish to wait, listen and encourage Dr. Boisen as he fought the inclination to relapse. There were religious people there as there always are in every hospital—doctors, nurses, social workers, attendants, other patients. But they were not able to share in the experience. When we need surgery we want a qualified surgeon; when we need car repairs we seek a mechanic; when we make a commercial flight we expect a skilled pilot to be at the controls. So, in the area of religion, when we are in despair we want the help of one who has studied the subject.

The pastor has studied religion and the ways of God and has a knowledge of those ways. He is expected to have mastered the truths about God in his mind and heart. Furthermore, through ordination, he is conferred with professional status by an official church body capable of judging his competency. The pastor symbolizes God, and the church, visible and invisible.

When Dr. Boisen began his work at the Worcester State Hospital there were no articles or books telling how a pastor could help the mentally ill. He later wrote some of these books, but he began by experimenting. He talked with patients and he listened. Some thanked him, and since it is the nature of mental illness, some laughed at him; others ignored him; some cursed him. But he understood. He had been there himself. He had cried, and laughed and cursed, but he had returned to health because he saw the vision of a cross in his hallucinations, a cross in the window; it is not surprising that a minister should have such thoughts in his illness, for in mental illness we see what we have seen in health; but there had been no one there to talk with him about it.

My illness was physical. Following a minor accident (an elbow bruise while swimming) I developed tuberculosis of the bone. Four years and two operations later the pain came in wave after wave; persistent, unrelenting, vicious and shattering—destroying my confidence, poise, hope and even my faith. I prayed, waited, cried, and cursed. After eleven days and nights when a second is a minute, a minute an hour, an hour a day, a day an eternity, the pain passed. But, my faith was gone. I had no words of gratitude, no prayer of thankfulness, no feelings of hope. There remained only disappointment, loneliness, anger; anger at God. I felt, I finally realized years later, God had rejected me. Like Boisen I experienced a deep sense of lostness. There was no man of God with whom to talk; no one to sit and wait and share my shattered thinking.

Three years later I went to the Massachusetts General Hospital to begin my work there. I had not read a single article or book on the subject of ministering to the sick. Some had been written in the last century, I learned later. These theorized that the pastor's task in the sick room is to prepare the patient for death, a preparation that was mechanical and rigid. No place was made for wonder and none for uncertainty.

Our former insights now seem simple and obvious. At first they were neither simple nor obvious; even now they are not simple although they are simply stated. Every pastor must test them himself and discover their reality for himself.

Basic Principles

Do no harm;	Make another appointment;
Supportive listening;	Refer to someone else;
Pastoral prayer;	Share your concern.

During the early weeks of my work at the Massachusetts General Hospital one of the social workers said to me, "I don't know whom you want to see, but we have a woman in my ward who I think should be seen by a minister. She is fifty-five, without funds, family, or friends, and she will never be able to work again. She may live two weeks and she may live two years. She's very discouraged."

I went to see the woman. She was lying in the corner bed in a ten-bed ward, with the curtains partially closed, crying quietly, a handkerchief held to her eyes. I introduced myself, saying, "I'm Mr. Dicks. Mrs. S., the social worker, told me you were here and I just dropped by to say, 'Hello.' " At the time I did not tell her I was a minister because I did not think it was important; perhaps I was reluctant to admit it. She motioned toward a chair at the bedside and began to talk; I listened and nodded, saying little. When I got up to leave twenty minutes later she was laughing. She said, "Thank you for coming to see me. I feel better." That was the first significant pastoral counseling interview that I had in the hospital; it lasted twenty minutes and I never saw the woman again for she left the hospital the next day. But there is no doubt that the conversation was helpful to her.

One day I found a statement in the *New England Journal of Medicine* which said, "The doctor's first principle in the care of the sick is to do no harm." When I called this to Dr. Cabot's attention he laughed. "Yes," he said, "if the doctor can avoid killing his patient through surgery or drugs most of them will get well." Later I understood why. Because God is working on the side of health.

"Do no harm" became our first principle in the sick room; and later in our pastoral counseling efforts beyond the sick room. There is always the risk, but at the same time I saw my first significant patient—the woman with heart disease who was weeping when I came and laughing when I left—my concern was to get in and get out without hurting her. "Thank you," she said, "I feel better." Was this our task—to help people to feel better? What has this to do with the kingdom of heaven? I asked. A great deal, I was later to learn, but for the time being I was content to have demonstrated the effectiveness of what came to be called "supportive listening," and which I formerly called "creative listening." Call it what you will, every experienced pastor discovers it for himself and then is mystified, saying, "All I did was listen."

A nurse from Hartford, Connecticut, with cancer of the lung came to the hospital as a patient. Two nights before the operation she asked that a minister be called. After I was seated at her bedside she said, "I know what I have and how serious the operation is. I also know the doctor can do only so much and that the patient must do the rest. I'm afraid I won't be able to do my part. That's why I wanted to see a pastor so that he can help me do my part."

The operation was unsuccessful.

Two weeks later as I stood at her bedside one night, she asked, "Do you think it will be tonight?" She referred to her approaching death.

I said, "I don't know. Do you think it will?"

"I don't know, but I want you to pray it will be. Only one thing more; I want you to come and be with my sister when it happens so she won't be alone." She died two nights later, and I learned the lesson of the importance of pastoral prayer, for it was through prayer, quiet prayers with eyes closed and her hand clasped tightly in mine that we groped for the strength she so desperately needed. Once she begged, "Stop by every time you are in this part of the building. I don't care if it's ten times a day." It was as many as four times in one day. Now she had the strength; now she looked forward with hope strong and sensitivities alert to death; death which had become for her an open door, not a blind alley.

Prayer by a pastor at the bedside, when he expresses the longing, the doubts, the hopes of the suffering person is a part of pastoral counseling also.

One day in Chicago, where I later served as chaplain of another hospital, my telephone rang. The frightened voice of a woman said she understood I talked with people who were in trouble. I set a time and she came to the office. She was approximately twenty-two, her hair was a bit untidy, her blouse a little dirty, her skirt a little wrinkled, and she was very nervous, but with it all she was a rather pretty girl. "How did you know about me?" I asked to break the ice and help her relax a little. She answered coolly, defensively, "I'd rather not say." I felt like going out and coming in again, as the students say when asked what they would do in a tough situation. So we started all over, but this time she talked while I waited.

She was a waitress, she explained, at a restaurant in Evanston. She had been having sexual intercourse with a Negro bus boy who also worked there. He had fallen in love with her and they planned to be married, but as they got close to the date she backed out and he had threatened to kill her. She was afraid of him because he had a violent temper.

Well . . . I thought and took a deep breath. . . . In pastoral counseling when in doubt grunt, when in doubt wait . . . A grunt seemed too aggressive, so I waited . . . and breathed. It turned out later that one of the theological students at Garrett Biblical Institute also worked at the same restaurant. He had observed that the girl was unduly nervous; when he inquired whether he might help her, she had declined his offer. He then explained that one of his professors, a chaplain in a downtown hospital, specialized in helping people in trouble, and that he was sure I would be glad to talk with her. Later the student told me about the girl and wondered why I did not tell him what was troubling her. (Keeping confidences is an essential part of pastoral counseling.)

"My life is all mixed up," she went on. "I've never been successful at anything."

"What do you mean?" I asked.

"Well, I've never been successful in my work, with my friends or in my love life, and I've never been successful in committing suicide."

A pastoral counselor must have curiosity, but he must keep it under control. This girl had already jarred me once, so it was not surprising that my guard was faulty.

"Just how have you tried to commit suicide?" I asked. Poor counseling; good curiosity; but a counselor is allowed, as in baseball, three strikes. That was my second one.

She said, "I've jumped into lakes, I've taken stuff, and I've jumped off buildings." Just behind me was a large, unscreened, open window, and my office was on the ninth floor.

"What was the highest building you ever jumped off?" I asked, and knew I should have waited for a better pitch.

She replied, "We don't have very tall buildings in Wisconsin."

But in counseling, as in baseball, we occasionally come to bat twice in one inning. I don't know what happened next, but I remember her story. It was the sordid, pathetic, tragic story of rejection and indifference by her parents—of having been in jail for three days when she was fourteen. When she told her parents, they said, "So what?" She left home. She had seen several psychiatrists at different times in the years that followed; she had been sectioned out of the Waves; she was often lonely. When she became lonely, she said, she went out on the street and picked up a man and had sexual intercourse. One man who lived in a nearby hotel had told her, after they had been to his room, that he did not think a nice girl should be taking such risks, and that whenever she wanted a man she should just come to him. No, she did not particularly enjoy intercourse because she never got satisfaction from it; but for a short time, however brief, she felt herself completely possessed (my words, her description).

What was she to do about her Negro boy friend? she asked. I did not know and told her so. I then followed another principle in pastoral counseling: I made another appointment for three days later. Taking a chance? Yes, but this girl's life had been lived on the ragged edge of chance.

She came for her appointment at the scheduled time. Her hair was still untidy, her blouse still dirty, her skirt still wrinkled, but she was different. There was a different look in her eye, a different tone in her voice. After seeing me she had talked with the boy. She had stood up to him, told him she would not marry, and that the affair was ended. He could do whatever he wished as she was no longer afraid of him. She was going to another town to see a woman who had once befriended her. She thanked me and left. She had gained strength for what she had to do, namely, break off wedding plans which would lead to disaster for her.

Is helping people gain strength the task of pastoral counseling? What has this to do with the kingdom of heaven? A great deal, for strength to face hard situations and make hard decisions is the doorway to the kingdom of heaven for many.

On another day, in Chicago, my telephone rang. The operator said, "San Antonio, Texas, calling." I waited, wondering who was calling and if I would be able to get away to make the speech they would be calling about. Suddenly over the telephone came the sound of Spanish. I thought, "I knew San Antonio would be given back to Mexico one of these days." But it was Mexico City calling, the call coming through San Antonio. It was an American businessman stationed there. His sister had secured my name from a pastor in South Carolina. His problem was that his wife had fallen in love with her nurse, and he was ready to kill both of them. What was he to do? We talked for twenty minutes. I advised him to come to Chicago where we could talk and where I could arrange for an appointment with a psychiatrist who knew something about homosexuality. He did. Eleven years later his sister called again, this time to refer a nephew who was having marital trouble. Her brother and his wife were still living together, she reported, and getting along reasonably well. They would like to see me, she was sure, if I ever went to Mexico City.

Referral is a part of pastoral counseling.

I said one day to a woman who sat rigidly upright in my counselee's chair, whose heart had been frozen years before, "You haven't had anyone be very kind to you for a long time, have you?" She had not wanted to come for counseling, but did so at her husband's insistence. The counseling had been tough going all the way. The story of her hostility was evident in her defense, her determined posture, the tone of her voice, and the listless resignation in the things she said. Now she stared at me as I said, "No one has been very kind to you for a long time." People had not meant to be unkind to her; I know, they never do. But, people do reach a point where they act out of desperation, ignorance and defiance. Suddenly, the heavens opened and the tears poured forth as she wept convulsively for minutes. Those words spoken in a moment of tenderness and understanding threw open a door to a new world that marked her rebirth. In the months that followed she gained strength to rebuild her life so that while she is still lonely she is a reasonably happy, busy, useful person.

In pastoral counseling we are not all things to all people. We accomplish very little with some and much with others. We don't solve problems; we help some people work out their problems, others to endure them, and still others to accept those which cannot be changed. And, we can seldom distinguish which is which. We instill our confidence in some and transmit our faith to others. We use words with some, prayers with others, and listening with all. Some need comfort; some need understanding; others need open affection, particularly those who are suffering grief in one form or another. In pastoral counseling we are certain that moralizing is of secondary importance. Of primary importance is courage and hope; courage to face problems and work at them, and confidence that tomorrow, next week or next month will be a better day.

TWO

The FIELD of PASTORAL CARE— CALLING

I. Pastoral Calling

The Pastor Goes to the People:
1. The Dying;
2. The Grief Suffering;
3. The Physically Ill;
4. The Shut-In;
5. The Older Person;
6. The Evangelistic Call;
7. The Routine Call.

II. Pastoral Counseling

The People Come to the Pastor:
1. Pre-marital Guidance;
2. Marriage Counseling;
3. The Alcoholic;
4. The Relative of the Alcoholic;
5. The Anxiety Sufferer;
6. The Depressive;
7. The Unwed Mother.

Here are fourteen different situations in which every pastor needs training, insight and skill. Church members rightly expect their pastors to minister effectively in each of these areas. Increasing demands are being made upon the modern minister in special cases relating to the homosexual, the dope addict and the sterile couple. Separate volumes on most of these subjects will be prepared for inclusion in this series. Other subjects will properly fall within the category of "the anxiety sufferer." In this chapter and the next we shall focus upon the fourteen most frequently encountered needs served in the pastoral ministry.

Pastoral Calling

1. **The Dying.** The mark of a great pastor, like a great physician, is the effectiveness of his care of the dying. Emotional ten-

sion seldom reaches a higher peak than at this transitional time when the seriously ill person faces death. This is the time when only religious hope is meaningful. In this crisis, doctor, nurse, pastor and trusted friend join hands to help both the patient and family. The doctor's task is to keep the patient free of pain and encourage him so that he may die with dignity. The nurse's task is to assist the doctor in her professional role and help the patient in any way she can. Many a patient draws heavily upon the nurse's courage, for dying is a lonely business. Fortunate, indeed, is the patient who, startled and delirious as he awakes, is reassured by the presence of a nurse, relative, pastor or friend.

The pastor permits the patient to talk as he wishes to, chats with him as he desires, prays as prayer is welcomed, lends strength to the patient's ebbing strength. Gradually the doors of faith are opened, patiently the paths of faith are trod; the realities of God become more real, the presence of God more supportive until the transition from life to death is one of ease. At such a time those who stand by can say, "Surely this one was a son of God," not *the* Son, but *a* son.

One seriously ill man said, "I am not afraid of death. I am afraid I won't die like a man."

Pastoral care demonstrates the truths proclaimed from the pulpit. The pivotal test of religious truth comes when death is imminent. Every effort should be made by the pastor to be present at the actual time of death.[1] This moment of death is a solemn occasion for all who are present. Certainly the pastor should be there. His prayer commending this loved one to the care of God and the benediction which closes such a prayer eases the rupture between man's time and eternity. Supportive friends find new faith, courage and hope. In quiet self-examination they rediscover fresh insight and outlook on death's mode and meaning.

2. **The Grief Sufferer.** Grief has been described as any broken interpersonal relationship. There is the grief we feel when a child starts to school. Many a mother would say, "Grief? You spell it r-e-l-i-e-f." Nevertheless, there is grief at knowing the little girl, the little boy, is now moving beyond the dependent state. Now the big girl, the big boy, turns to others.

[1] A volume on *"Ministering to the Dying"* will follow in this series by Carl J. Scherzer, Chaplain of the Protestant Deaconess Hospital, Evansville, Indiana.

There is the grief one feels when a son or daughter goes away to college; joy, but grief also. There are the feelings of grief that parents know when a son or daughter goes into military service, and when they marry. There is the grief one feels in separation and divorce—a broken interpersonal relationship—when one is faced with loneliness and a sense of failure. The grief the pastor faces consistently and which calls for his devoted attention is the grief felt by parishioners following the death of a loved one. He should be sensitive to the other situations, but he *must* give attention to this one. In my opinion more people are lost to the church, more carry life-long resentment toward God, because of pastoral failure in the ministry to grief-suffering persons than for any other reason.

The religions of all three faiths in our culture, Roman Catholicism, Judaism and Protestantism in almost all of its branches, have taught that God determines the precise moment of death for each person, that death takes place at that time regardless of what we do. Actual facts contradict such belief. Nevertheless, it has clung to generation after generation. How easy it is to ignore scientific advances that prolong life, and safety rules that protect life. When a loved one dies, we say, "God took him," and we are angry. Yet, if we truly believed that statement, we would joyfully say, "How fortunate that he is with God!" But who would listen and share in this joy? Who would listen to one talk of God in time of sadness? Who feels secure enough in his own belief to let another express anger? The pastor must. If he does not, the suffering increases and the doubt becomes chronic. It is important that he avoid trying to win arguments about God in the face of grief. Grief time is a time to share tenderness and demonstrate hope, since the grief-stricken are then more responsive to pastoral care than at any other time.

Eric Linderman, M.D., psychiatrist, became interested in the study of grief reactions shortly before World War II following Boston's Coconut Grove night club disaster in which several hundred persons were killed or injured. It was observed that many of the injured who had lost loved ones in the fire failed to respond to medical treatment. Dr. Linderman was called in consultation, and later continued his interest in the subject. He eventually concluded that each person suffering from grief needs from six to ten hours of somebody's *listening* time to overcome his grief feelings after a death. If he does not get that time, his melancholy will continue and sometimes he will remain ill.

3. **The Physically Ill.** There is more to physical illness than discomfort and pain. An imbalance may be observed in terms of anxiety, uncertainty, doubt and rejection feelings. Coupled with this strange new imbalance of body and mind is the patient's need to adjust to hospitalization.

Following admission to the hospital, the patient finds himself surrounded by unfamiliar equipment, strange procedures and strange people. Some patients quickly succeed in adjusting to the "ritual," but there are still the moments of loneliness and impatient watching and waiting; especially when visiting hours have ended. It is during these hours that the pastor's call can be most helpful in restoring the patient's perspective. With quiet calm and in an unhurried, but not unduly extended, visit, the pastor brings new hope and confidence to the patient.

Today, most hospital authorities welcome the pastor as a member of the health team. It is for that reason that he is permitted to call at any hour of the day or night. Indeed, most hospital administrators prefer that he make his regular calls outside the so-called "visiting hours." In this unique and specialized role, the pastor's first concern is to minister to the specific needs of the person. If he is to effectively do so, it will be necessary to clearly understand the patient's inner feelings. Only after establishing that base of operation is it possible to proceed with skill and assurance. One must begin at the hub of the patient's mental, emotional and spiritual make-up.[2]

Within the period of illness there are clearly defined crises points that must be kept in mind. Each has its peculiar problems and calls for discernment. Crises areas include: (a) *Pre-Surgical Care:* a surgical operation is an act of faith—the patient trusts the doctor, the anesthetist, the hospital equipment, and the sustaining power of God; every patient prays to the best of his ability before surgery; (b) *Accepting Physical Handicaps:* after illness or injury, such as limited activity following a heart attack; (c) *Protracted Convalescence:* where time and boredom wear heavily, depress, rob one of hope and undermine confidence; (d) *Serious Illness:* discussed earlier under the topic of dying.

[2] See chapter 13 in *The Art of Ministering to the Sick.*

Every such situation calls for special effort, attention and time on the part of the pastor. The minister and doctor need to work closely together in these crises. It is not so important that a pastor know a patient's diagnosis as it is that he know if there are special problems with which he should be familiar. A telephone call to the doctor saying, "I am Mr. Blank, a minister. You are taking care of Mrs.—, who is one of my parishioners. Is there anything I should know to be of help to her?" This will establish a doctor's confidence in a pastor and often there will be some special problem that is vital to a patient's recovery. Here the sensitive and understanding pastor can help where others could not. Every physician would prefer to work with a patient who has faith rather than one who is controlled by anxiety. The physician observes that the faithful respond better to treatment, makes better recoveries, are more pleasant, more grateful—and pay their bills.

4. **The Shut-In.** The shut-in is one whose activity is limited to house, wheel chair, or bed. Radio and television have done much to break the monotony, but the basic problem remains. An odd dilemma confronts the shut-in. In normal living there is never sufficient time. The shut-in has time, but most shut-ins find it heavy, slow-moving and meaningless. While they may have the radio, television, books, handiwork, they miss companionship. More than that, they feel they have lost control of their time and, therefore, the structure for purposeful living.

Pastoral care of the shut-in is very likely to become routine calling. Ideally, it should be guided visiting or what I would call, "disciplined conversation." It should seek to probe the inner thoughts of the parishioner. If there is little reflective thinking, the pastor often can stimulate it by discussing books, ideas, or other articles of interest.

Sometimes, of course, the pastor can encourage a shut-in person to use his time constructively even to the point of rehabilitation. There are now extensive programs of self-education and self-help. However, with all these efforts there are still a few people who will remain shut in; many of these have or could have active minds. Others simply wait out time finding it tedious and dreadful. Here the pastor draws upon his own faith and his belief that such existence is contrary to the desires of God and one is not content until purpose can be found for such a person. Here your patience, your imagina tion, and your dedication as a pastor will be tested as at few other points.

5. **The Older Person.** Older people often become shut-ins or semi-shut-ins and need special attention. Here again the great problem is time and the meaningfulness of time. With the upward trend of life expectancy this problem will increase. Paul Dudley White, the eminent heart specialist, recently said that it is reasonable to expect people to live "happily" to one hundred years of age. Note that he said *happily*. It is not enough to live to advanced years, sickly, disgruntled, or with a sour disposition. Rather, one must strive to live enthusiastically, hopefully and with contentment. Years are being added to life; can life be added to years? Income, health, housing, companionship, attitude or outlook (psychological and philosophical) are the major problems of senior citizens. The church can do little about the first three; although constant and increased efforts are successfully being made to establish more church sponsored homes for older people. Still, the total problem is almost untouched by these efforts.

In considering the senior citizen the church must direct its major attention to the problems of attitude—to assist people to handle their advancing years in more meaningful ways. America is wasting one of its greatest resources: the wisdom of its senior citizens. Their insights, wisdom and leadership could easily be harnessed by church and society. The great need is that we understand this fundamental fact, believe it, and act accordingly.

When the pastor calls upon older persons, he does a lot of listening and a lot of encouraging. Often he goes away from such a call refreshed in spirit for he has been in communion with one who, through the experience of life, has known deep things of the soul. Such calls are not difficult and the busy pastor's inclination is to neglect them; then the necessity for an orderly and planned schedule of calling becomes apparent, for the pastor must not overlook anyone.

6. **The Evangelistic Call.** Our Lord's method of evangelism was through direct contact. He spoke with people in all stations of life asking questions and answering them. And, he listened. People are isolated from each other and, as their feeling of isolation grows, they feel isolated from God. Most are familiar with the message of religion and many are familiar with the particular doctrines of each

church, at least in a general way. The acceptance, understanding and affection that a church practices is ultimately of greater importance than its doctrinal standards. The church in all its branches is in the business of redemption, of salvation. It goes about this business in many ways. By and large it consistently attempts to shift a person's preoccupation with himself and his problems to a faith in a power greater than himself. Religion does not say (some do, unfortunately, for almost anything is said sooner or later in the name of religion), "God will solve your problems, you have nothing to worry about." Rather, religion says, "You are not alone." Religion seeks not only to establish faith in God but it seeks to build hope—hope of many kinds—that the world in which we live is creative, that one's fellow creatures, while given to human frailties, are trustworthy, that life is worthwhile. Religion seeks to build bridges of communication between people. Sometimes the bridge becomes a drawbridge that always seems to be up, but, in season and out, religion seeks to increase tolerance toward other people who may be different from one's self and whose ideas do not agree with our own. In this latter it often fails.

These beliefs and many others, the church seeks to propagate. Evangelism in our day is finding one's way to people and demonstrating concern and affection for those people. The church is often described as "the fellowship of the concerned." Evangelism extends that concern to people outside the fellowship. The intention is not to entice them into the fellowship for selfish reasons relating to prestige, growth and financial support. The purpose of evangelism is to demonstrate the concern of the fellowship because it is the nature of one who feels concern to share love with others. (See Chapter 5) It is not my intention here to discuss the *how* of evangelism but only to point out that evangelism in our day is usually an individual person to person, face to face conversation matter, even when a church carries on special evangelistic services once a year, and as such falls under the head of pastoral work. It often grows out of effective ministry to the sick, the convalescent, the dying, the grief suffering, helpfulness in marriage counseling, or other areas of distress.

7. **The Routine Call.** So far as I know this is my own term for that call which in the church has been traditionally described as "visiting." I have never liked the term "visiting" for it implies, "You

tell one and I'll tell one" which is light, chatty, impersonal, and while pleasant, may gloss over feelings and ignore anxieties. The pastor may visit, but his task is not just to visit; his tools may include visiting but he has far more important techniques at his command.

By definition the routine call is that call by the pastor upon a parishioner for no other reason than that this person is a member of your church. (Note: I say, *parishioner*—if the call is made upon a non-parishioner it is an evangelistic call whether or not the church, Christ, God or commitment is even mentioned.) That is why a call upon a member of another church while he is sick is proselytizing and is as unethical as one doctor examining and prescribing for another doctor's patient. It does not matter how prominent either the patient or the pastor is in the community. If the call is made upon a sick or grief-stricken relative of a parishioner, it is still an evangelistic call.

The routine call is generally neglected by pastors due to their busy schedules and because it is hard to find people at home. Even so, this kind of calling is as important as any the minister does. This call makes contact, builds confidence, establishes a relationship, opens doors. Some years ago I was teaching in the summer sessions at the Iliff School of Theology, Denver, Colorado. One of the assignments in the class in Pastoral Care required each student to report a routine call. A student serving a church in western Kansas was irritated by the assignment saying that he had no time for such calls. The assignment stood. He reported a call upon a family, the Browns, in his church who were inactive members. They welcomed him, but avoided his attempts to discuss their absence from worship. During the course of the call, the sixteen-year-old son of the family came in with a string of fish he had just caught. Everyone got up to admire them. My student in his written evaluation of the call wrote, "The most religious thing I did during my call on the Browns was look at the fish." In my comment on his paper I wrote, "Could be."

Two weeks later, the student sheepishly handed in another report. Six days after his routine call, as he returned to his parsonage, a waiting neighbor said, "You'd better get over to the Browns. Their son was just struck and killed by lightning an hour ago while driving a tractor." Now the minister went into a grief-stricken home as a pastor and friend, not as a stranger who had shown no interest in them.

The routine call often brings out trouble that is not known to the minister before the call. In my classes in the theological seminary with students serving churches we found that the routine call turned up crisis material in approximately thirty per cent of the calls and sometimes as high as forty, depending upon the maturity of the student.

Dr. Karl Menninger has called the pastor "the poor man's psychiatrist." Counseling is often started in the routine call because there the relationship is established not as preacher-parishioner, nor as leader-worshiper, but as pastor-parishioner or counselor-counselee.

The minister is different from any other professional counselor. He moves into town on Thursday, earlier in the week if possible, and by the following Monday is in business, earlier if he follows a pastoral minded minister. Soon after arriving he inquires of a leading layman if there are any known seriously ill people in the parish. If his predecessor has been careful and if his leaving is not too long removed (here the Methodist system works best, for one minister leaves and another arrives the same day), the departing minister will have left a list of the critically ill, the recently bereaved, within three months to a year, the ill, both physically and mentally, the alcoholics with whom he has been working, the shut-ins, and others who need early attention, such as parents of a handicapped child. These persons, in the order of their listing, should have priority upon the minister's calling time.

As soon as he has covered this list, early in the second week of his stay in a new church, the minister should call upon the official members of the board, the officers of the Women's Society, the youth groups, the key leaders in the Sunday School. After these calls he is ready to start his routine calling. It is to be hoped the minister will arrive with enough sermons to carry him for a few weeks so that he can devote a major amount of energy to calling for soon his time will be claimed by organization work, study and counseling. Time should be allotted for routine calling in addition to the calling required in the major categories listed above.[3] If the church is large, the problem

[3] See *How To Make Pastoral Calls for Ministers and Laymen,* Russell L. Dicks (St. Louis, The Bethany Press, 1962).

becomes more complicated and the pastor must have help, sometimes a great deal of help.

The minister should explain to the chairman of the board, and perhaps the Pastoral Relations Committee, the plan of calling which he will follow, lest some touchy elder or deacon may get his feelings hurt. A simple explanation will avoid unnecessary risk. Some pastors follow the practice of stating, simply and briefly, their calling plan the first Sunday in the pulpit when they are expressing their greetings to the congregation. This would be a strategic time to touch lightly upon formal counseling.

Some years ago I was lecturing upon pastoral care at a Minister's Convocation at Howard University in Washington, D.C. In the forum one of the ministers got carried away in his conception of the enormity of the pastoral task. He got up presumably to ask a question, but made a speech, instead, ending his remarks with, "Thank God for sin! I'll have a job until I die." No church is so small that the pastor could not have time used to its fullest "until he dies," if he likes people and works at the pastoral job. Routine calling is the cornerstone of good pastoral care.

THREE

The FIELD of PASTORAL CARE— COUNSELING

Pastoral Counseling

1. Pre-marital Guidance;
2. Marriage Counseling;
3. The Alcoholic;
4. The Relative of the Alcoholic;
5. The Anxiety Sufferer;
6. The Depressive;
7. The Girl Pregnant Out of Wedlock.

Separate volumes in the series will relate to these subjects. Our immediate purpose is to establish boundary lines so that the pastor might see their proportionate relationship to his total parish ministry. With the multiple demands upon the minister, this may appear to be an impossible task. Furthermore, many of these conditions call for expert handling and for skills and time that most local pastors do not have. Nevertheless, the minister needs practical guides to deepen his insights and broaden his outlook in these areas where people need direction, counseling and, frequently, referral.

1. **Pre-marital Guidance.** What was called pre-marital counseling a generation ago is now rightly referred to as Pre-marital Guidance. Today's need is one of instruction rather than counseling. On occasion, this instruction may revert to counseling, provided the pastor encounters anxiety or tensions that require protracted and confidential sessions. Ordinarily, pre-marital guidance deals with facts and appropriate instruction and discussion.

In his pastoral role, the minister is frequently called upon to officiate at weddings. Unlike the civil servant, legally authorized to perform a marriage, the pastor acts with and beyond that same legal authorization. In a unique way, he seals the marriage relationship with the blessing of God and the church upon the marriage partners and the home to be established.

Most marriages involve members of the pastor's own parish. But, there are also the occasional non-members who desire the blessing of the church upon their union. In either instance, there will be times when the minister must face the issue of divorce and remarriage. With a rising divorce rate, this problem will recur more frequently.

Some church bodies have an ironclad rule forbidding the remarriage of any divorced person. Others permit the remarriage of the "innocent" party to a divorce. Still others allow the pastor to decide the matter on the basis of the particular circumstances involved in the dissolution of the prior marriage. One's procedure will necessarily be governed by the discipline and practice of his church body and its polity.

Apart from such considerations, there are basic factors worthy of the pastor's consideration. A strong defense could be made for the pastoral obligation to marry any member of the parish, even though he may have had a previous marriage failure. To refuse to do so would amount to downgrading church membership. The very act of denial would amount to rejection. Such judgment on the part of pastor and church body discounts the spirit of forgiveness and denies the petitioner the right to the spiritual blessing he seeks.

The answer to marital tragedy is not to be found in refusal and rejection. Many pastors find that the occasion of remarriage offers them an opportunity to provide guidance. They can now offer help and hope in areas of human relationships where it is quite possible that the church has failed to minister effectively to the parties of the first marriage. Here, then, is a renewed opportunity for better marital guidance.

While other professional people, the doctor, social worker and psychology marriage counselors may do pre-marital guidance work, the clergy will do ninety to ninety-five per cent of whatever is done because of the position pastors occupy in the church and community.

Actually, the pastor smuggles in his pre-marital guidance, for a couple has come to him simply to seek a sacrament, a service, a ceremony. However, almost all engaged couples want all the help they can find to make their marriage successful. The problem is one of available pastoral time and energy. How does one have the time necessary to give the desired instruction? The pastor who performs many weddings should have an established class of instruction for those about to be married. This need not be limited to those who have set a wedding date or even to those who have chosen a mate. Neither should it be limited only to those who are looking toward marriage. Frequently, it is possible to include recently married couples who missed the instruction class. It is inadvisable to admit people who are having serious marriage problems. These should go into a marriage counseling group.

It should be made clear in the instruction class that those who feel the need to discuss specific problems, such as an overly protective parent, should make an appointment with the pastor for individual counseling. An unnecessary amount of time may be spent with one couple with a problem that does not affect the others. Also, instruction will not deal with anxiety; that calls for counseling.

I do not visualize this class as being a full course upon marriage and the family, such as is often offered in churches to young people. It is more like the instruction that is carried on with individual couples before marriage. It covers such questions as budget, church affiliation (for not all will be members of the same church), sexual happiness. The latter should be dealt with in detail using such aids as the *Sex Knowledge Inventory*[1] and such books as *Sex Without Fear*[2] and *Modern Sex Techniques*.[3] The instruction should end with a detailed examination of the wedding ceremony itself, very much as you would in counseling with an individual couple. This same material should be covered in individual instruction if you have no class but it would be more helpful when presented to a group, for various questions, helpful to all, will be asked. Special care should be taken by the pastor to be certain that levity and wisecracks by the inevitable wit in the class does not effect the seriousness of the presentation. In fact, each session should be opened with a prayer to insure the note of seriousness and dignity of the instruction. I can imagine few subjects more serious. A physician may be used if one is available to discuss the subject of planned parenthood, but he

[1] Family Life Publications, Inc., College Station, Durham, North Carolina.
[2] Medical Research Press, 136 West 52 Street, New York 19, New York.
[3] Lancer Books, 26 West 47 Street, New York 36, New York.

should not be asked to discuss sexual relations as few doctors communicate well on this subject and there is nothing in his training that particularly prepares him as an authority upon sex act techniques. However, if he does some marriage counseling, he will be able to make a contribution.

The young and inexperienced pastor, particularly the unmarried minister, may want to arrange with a more mature man to substitute for him at this phase of the instruction. Many instances have come to my attention of young ministers who were severely criticized by prudish parishioners frightened at the material and books being discussed in pre-marital guidance. Such critics are often emotionally disturbed. Nevertheless, they can and do cause serious trouble. There is no point in a young pastor endangering his career when with forethought and planning it can be avoided.

2. **Marriage Counseling.** One of the most rapidly expanding subjects in pastoral care is marriage counseling. The whole field of marriage and the family has developed significantly in the past few years. Popular writers and commentators upon marriage and family problems constantly recommend that people with marriage problems talk to counselors and pastors. While many people conceal their marital difficulties from their ministers, still others go first to the pastor, even though he may be untrained in marriage counseling. More often than not, the minister has no one in his community to whom he can refer a couple. He must, therefore, do the best he can. It is because of our recognition of the seriousness of this subject that *Marital Counseling* was one of the first books planned in this series.[4]

No one is very certain as to why we are faced with a growing crisis in the family in America. I believe that marriage is undergoing a social revolution. The liberation of women dates back to World War II. Woman has since become economically free. She can now enter almost any profession and trade and support herself. Labor-saving devices have freed her from household drudgery. She is free also from the sexual domination of man. No longer is she convinced that sex is "something you put up with for the sake of being married." Modern women now insist that sexual happiness is an integral part of marriage. Without that adjustment, marriage is a failure. We do

[4] See *Marital Counseling* by Dr. R. Lofton Hudson (Prentice-Hall, Inc., Englewood Cliffs, New Jersey, 1963).

not find women actually seeking divorce on the basis of these newly-found freedoms. The ostensible reason is mental cruelty. Yet, through economic freedom, women no longer have to tolerate the cruelty of thoughtless and sadistic husbands.

We are also discovering that children are hurt more by quarreling and bickering within the home than by a divided home. In a study by William J. Goode[5] of Columbia University, of 425 divorced women two years after divorce 31 per cent reported they felt their children were happier than before the divorce, 9 per cent felt the divorce had been bad for the child, while 10 per cent could see no effect whatsoever. The others fell into various categories such as "worried because of lack of a father (not necessarily the divorced father), mother worried about social stigma, religious rejection."

Of the teen-agers seen in our Counseling Center during the past year with emotional disturbances, 70 per cent were living in homes where there was conflict and where the parents were living together. These children were referred by the juvenile court, pastors, doctors, or brought in by parents because of running away from home, poor school work, incorrigibility, disobedience and extreme anxiety. This supports the growing belief among marriage and family counselors that conflict in the home, not divorce as such, does the damage.

"From the point of view of children we are beginning to realize that the way a divorce is arrived at can do much to modify the hurt. . . . The modern approach is not to preserve the (legal) family at all costs, but to promote the adequacy and satisfaction of family members in and through marriage. . . . One does not preserve the values of marriage merely by preserving the form."[6]

Marriage is the joining of the wills and desires of two people in companionship, communication, concern, and affection so that the feelings they share overflow into the lives of their children and others they meet. It is a permissive relationship, not held together by force, threat or pressure. The desire for marriage is the desire for companionship and love. When this desire is frustrated, the marriage turns to destruction.

A destructive marriage is one where the relationship has turned

[5] *After Divorce* (Glencoe, Illinois, Free Press, 1956) page 317.
[6] *Marriage Counseling, A Casebook* (New York, Association Press, 1958) pages 27–28.

from love to hate, from concern to indifference, from shared feelings of encouragement to bitter feelings of nagging. Instead of mutual self confidence where the persons involved feel they can face the world with courage and dignity, there are feelings of bitterness, anger, and hopelessness. These negative feelings must be resolved and converted to affection lest one, two, or more lives be saddened, if not crippled. The minister, in and out of homes, as close as the telephone, understanding and non-judgmental, is the most available helping person in the community. To be helpful he must be objective, disciplined and concerned.

Whenever possible, however, the local pastor would do well to refer couples to the professionally trained marriage counselor. His special training and skills, the time he can devote to the interviews, and the professional nature of this service; all contribute to a more effective handling of serious marital problems. In this setting, the distraught couple can vent feelings they would probably conceal from the minister. Thus, the sessions are likely to probe more deeply and proceed more rapidly in this objective, impersonal and fee basis counseling situation.

3. **The Alcoholic.** Here again we are confronted with a subject of urgency. For this reason, a book upon ministry to the alcoholic has been prepared by The Reverend Thomas J. Shipp of Dallas, Texas.[7] "Tom" Shipp helped introduce the Alcoholics Anonymous program to Dallas and has continued to exert a marked influence upon the organization there. Confronted with the task of helping alcoholics, Tom learned the hard way. Untold numbers of men and women owe their sobriety, their homes, their way of life, and life itself, directly or indirectly to the judgment, devotion and friendship of Tom Shipp.

Alcoholism is a sickness; one of the most stubborn and resistive illnesses which we see—surpassed in difficulty only by drug addiction. More and more people are trapped by it each year. While alcoholism results from excessive drinking of alcoholic beverages, the underlying causes are multiple. Accordingly, we say that alcoholism is a symptom of other problems. Regardless of the underlying causes, alcoholism is a major problem in society today.

Alcoholism is a sickness unto death, inasmuch as the alcoholic is

[7] *Helping the Alcoholic and His Family*, by Thomas J. Shipp (Prentice-Hall, Inc., Englewood Cliffs, New Jersey, 1963).

in a sense trying to kill himself. He may not know or admit this truth. In the course of time, whether it be brief or extended, alcohol will destroy a person, either directly or indirectly.

The disease of alcoholism is self-inflicted, since no one can be forced to drink. The first decision to drink is volitional. Only later on does it become compulsive. At that point, a man is as helpless as if he were in a strait jacket—until he determines to free himself.

There is hope for the alcoholic. When he truly wants to stop drinking, he can. This can be done not solely by self-will, but through the combined assistance of concerned people who rally to support the alcoholic's determination. No one, but no one, can force the alcoholic to stop drinking except under the controlled situation of his hospitalization. The only reliable controlling force is one's inner resolution.

Alcoholics Anonymous is responsible for more people controlling their addiction to alcohol than any other effort. Just how A.A. achieves its results is not very clear. Its program is essentially religious; its twelve steps being drawn from religion. The minister, unless he is an alcoholic himself, plays a supportive, encouraging role in A.A. Many A.A.'s find a welcome place in the life of the church and become active church leaders. The non-drinking alcoholic, a compulsive person by nature, is determined and enthusiastic. It is a common observation that one may then find him as hard at work in a church program as he was in his previous days of excessive drinking.

Often, the alcoholic must be taken to a hospital or sobering-up place when his body has become debilitated. The minister may be the one who convinces him to go and receive treatment. Rather than struggle with a person and a problem he little understands, the minister is well advised to have some A.A. members work with the alcoholic when he is ready and willing to accept help.

4. **The Relative of the Alcoholic.** The minister plays an important role with the relative of the alcoholic. He is in a position to hold the family together or encourage the wife to leave. A wife clings to her marriage with mixed feelings of pity, anxiety and guilt. Despite the broken resolutions of her alcoholic spouse, she clings to the hope that he will reverse his course and return to sobriety. A wife's loyalty to such a marriage often represents her dependency rather than

her desire to help the husband. The decision to preserve the marriage should be based upon the children's rights and well-being and the behavior pattern of the husband when drunk. Sometimes the fear of marital separation will shock the alcoholic into sober reflection. Alcoholics frequently threaten to commit suicide. The A.A.'s laugh at such threats, saying it is par for the course and an old trick of the alcoholic.

Whatever the decision and whatever the course of action, the relative should be put in touch with the Alanon Club, sister organization to Alcoholics Anonymous, made up of wives of alcoholics. They will help the relative to understand how he or she is contributing to the drinking problem. Understanding and maturity of the nondrinking mate is vitally important.

Encourage the wife or husband to be cautious about threats to leave home. Once a threat is made, it should be followed through. I talked one wife into permitting her husband to bring his alcohol into the house. He customarily kept a bottle in the garage. It was his house, I told her, and she should either let him drink in the house or they should separate. He would not believe his wife when she told him she would not pour out his liquor, so he kept his usual bottle in the garage having a nip when he parked his car and another when he got in the house. So our problem instead of lessening, doubled. It was necessary to have a conference with both of them together, as it was still a good idea to put him on his own responsibility.

The average minister will know little about the subject of alcoholism when he starts his work. Read books on the subject, attend A.A. meetings, enroll in courses that are offered in pastors' schools, start working with one or two alcoholics and their families; keep your ears open and your mouth shut. Alcoholics will teach you how to help them but be prepared to give of yourself and your affection. If you can, the rewards will be as great as any pastoral effort you will ever make.

5. **The Anxiety Sufferer.**[8] This is a general category to cover that type of person who does things the hard way, who runs ahead to every crisis and finds crises where there are none, who, as Shake-

[8] See *Ministering to the Mentally Ill,* Ernest E. Bruder (Prentice-Hall, Inc., Englewood Cliffs, New Jersey, 1963).

speare said, "finds a bush a bear." These people are worriers, but their worries are not to be taken lightly as their suffering is as real as those who suffer from known causes.

Ours has been called "the age of anxiety" just as it is increasingly called "the age of tranquillizers." We are surrounded by bigness and no time in history was ever geared to make man more fully conscious of that bigness than ours. Big business, big labor, big government, big taxes, big transportation, big communication, big politics, big propaganda, big bombs, big wars, big destruction . . . and we are so little, so insignificant, so helpless. What can we do as bigness tightens the ring around us? Threats, warnings, and fears surround us! Take pills, take tranquillizers, build bomb shelters, and then be told almost before the plans for the shelter are drawn that it is obsolete. While we cannot be sure that the anxiety of our day is directly traceable to power politics and threats of nuclear war, we are certainly not immune from the undercurrent of such latent fears.

Some people seem to draw their tendency to worry directly from their parents, particularly their mothers. A famous psychiatrist wrote a book in which he maintained that the world's problems could be laid at the feet of women, saying that children take their emotions from their mothers. Children are fearful or courageous in direct ratio to their mothers' actions, since their mothers directly influence their formative years.

A strong case could be made to prove the opposite. Knowing how dependent wives are upon their husbands, particularly during the time of pregnancy and child rearing, it could be argued that the emotional stability of the family is rooted in the strength or weakness of the father. If fathers are kind, they are kind; if fathers are harsh, they are fearful. When fathers are indifferent, they become anxious and these emotions are transmitted to the children. Actually, there will be exceptions to the rule. Some wives rise above the injustices in their marriage relationship; they rise above the whimsies, moods, affections or rejections of their husbands just as some children become stronger and healthier emotionally than the home from which they come. Otherwise, there would be little change from generation to generation; the rigidities of behavioristic determinism would be even greater than that ascribed to by some theologians of the past who denied all freedom of will. There is a large place for heroism.

The anxiety sufferer of a compulsive nature may wash his hands over and over again (which is often a sign of unrecognized guilt feelings). He may follow rituals of thinking and acting–much as a doctor in Chicago, who felt compelled to dissect the manhole cover in front of his office building by riding squarely over it with the right hand front wheel of his car whenever he came to his office. At times, he would drive around the block several times to accomplish this, and upon arriving in his office he would go to the sink, wash his hands, dry them upon a towel which his nurse must hand him in an exact same way every morning, spit over his left shoulder, and then go to work. This doctor would have no further difficulty as there were no further rituals of action required through the day. But, the next day he must follow the same procedure. On days he did not come to the office, all ritual was off.

Neurotic anxiety, persistent, resistive, and stubborn, goes on and on and people learn to live with it. The pastor is baffled, frustrated, often angered by such behavior. I advise referral for these people so that they may be managed by therapists with deeper psychological insights than those of the pastor. You must listen to them for two to three hours spread over as many weeks; if there is no improvement: refer. Refer first to the local physician and follow through with him. Tranquillizers will sometimes help. Often they will not, and then a person is back to you. Ask permission to call the physician. Some doctors may become impatient with such people, particularly those with limited knowledge of psychiatry. On occasion, they may storm and pull rank both on the sufferer and the pastor instead of honestly admitting that there is no known successful treatment for such a person. Professional fees paid by anxiety-ridden people support the psychoanalysts, psychiatrists and sometimes the non-medical counselor. Sometimes they improve, but usually they go on suffering and worrying. Be as cheerful as you can, but try not to jump off the bridge with them.

6. **The Depressive.** Depression is the most common type of mental disturbance. There is some measure of depression with other types of illnesses. The symptoms of depression are similar to some of those of acute anxiety, so that care should be taken to check them out

for the depressed person is a potential suicide risk. I write of it here simply to introduce the pastor to the subject, and urge that serious attention be given to further study. The depressed person feels guilty and, therefore, he brings his guilt problems to the pastor. Furthermore, he is afraid he will hurt himself and comes to the pastor because of that fear. Being frightened and guilty he turns to the most accessible person in the community: the pastor.

The symptoms of depression are: (1) Tearfulness or crying (found also in anxiety); (2) Loss of appetite, loss of sleep, loss of weight; (3) Slowness or sluggishness of speech; (4) Rapid onset of the condition–if a person reports he has "always felt this way" he is an anxiety sufferer, although some depressions go on for several years; (5) Self depreciation which may involve suicidal reference–do not hesitate to inquire if a depressed person feels life is not worthwhile, and whether he has had thoughts of self-destruction. You need not fear that this will suggest suicide to him; (6) Loss of sex interest; (7) References to the unpardonable sin; (8) There is no known situation to account for his feelings, such as recent grief experience; (9) Previous similar experience.

Depressive illness tends to recur. It is wise to ask a person, "Did you ever have this kind of depression before?" A person will frequently answer, "Well, yes, but it was different . . . not like this." Close questioning will bring out the fact, however, that it was not very different from the present one. If the depression seems heavy and the counselee has difficulty describing previous episodes, it is wise for the minister to question the family, inquiring if they recall or know of similar experiences in a person's life.

The minister should not try to evaluate a person as to whether or not he will commit suicide. Even well-trained psychiatrists hesitate to make such a judgment. When in doubt call the local physician.

Closely associated with the mood of depression, but on the opposing end of the scale is elation and enthusiasm without obvious cause. The elated condition does not always proceed or follow depression, but it is not uncommon for a person to quickly vacillate from one mood to the other. The elated person may be very persuasive. A medical resident at a hospital where I served rose to a state of elation where he proceeded to buy an apartment house without cash or collateral. I knew of another elated man who bought a string of trucks to the amazement of his wife and father when he did not have enough cash to buy a tank of gas. An elated person has tremendous powers of persuasion.

Both depression and elation are treated with tranquillizers and in extreme instances with electric or insulin shock. The minister can be of great help to the family and counselee by assuring them that the depressed or elated person will recover. These persons *always get well.* He should, however, work closely with a physician, and not personally assume the responsibility for the welfare of such a person.

7. **The Girl Pregnant Out of Wedlock.** The minister is often consulted by the girl who becomes pregnant out of wedlock. Sometimes he is consulted by her parents. Here the pastor is in position to be of great help; first, in helping a girl with her guilt feelings; secondly, by helping her and her family shape up a plan for her care; and third, by helping the family accept the situation.

There are four ways to handling this problem: (1) Abortion; (2) Marriage; (3) Raising the child out of wedlock by the mother or relative; (4) Placing the child for adoption.

(1) Abortion is illegal and dangerous because it is often done under unhygienic conditions by untrained and unprincipled people who take few, if any, precautions against the risk of infection. It should be discouraged by the minister. If an abortion has already been performed or attempted and the counselee reports pain and bleeding, she should be gotten to a doctor at once. (2) Marriage is the old-fashioned solution to this problem and one which is still practiced by many. In my marriage counseling, I see many couples who were married because of premarital pregnancy. Their marriages are in trouble because they began with resentment. If a couple is in love and had planned marriage before the pregnancy, then getting married even if the date is moved up may be desirable. Otherwise, marriage is not the recommended solution. Tremendous pressure may be brought upon a boy to do the "right thing," and the minister who counsels against the marriage is on the spot. (3) Raising the child out of wedlock places a stigma upon both the mother and child even though it is raised by the mother's parents or relatives. It seldom quite comes off. Although tremendous love may be given the child, there is

still a feeling of being different. And, there is often an attitude of "you made your bed now lie in it" attitude toward the mother. The claim of many a girl, "I cannot give up my baby," is both sentimental and immature. A mother develops her love for a baby by caring for it, not by conceiving and having it. The pastor should avoid arguing with a girl under these circumstances. At the same time, he ought not to acquiesce to her tearful plea. (4) Placing the baby for adoption is by all odds the best solution to this problem. In this way the baby gets a break for it is placed in a home of love and usually of comfort with people who are well able to give it care and an education. The child's mother is not stigmatized, and she can resume her life again, more mature for the experience and often much wiser. There are far more childless couples seeking babies than there are babies available for adoption. In fact, one out of seven couples are unable to conceive children. I recently heard of a couple who adopted two children and then, as so often happens, had one of their own. The older children were greatly concerned that the baby was not adopted as they had been. One said, "Mother, couldn't we adopt her and then she need never know the difference?"

In advising the placing of a baby for adoption the pastor should work closely with a recognized and approved adoption agency. In fact, the expectant mother should go to a home wherever possible, such as Salvation Army or Florence Crittenton Home. If this is not possible, she may go to a relative or friend in another city and have her baby there.

It is believed by some social workers that girls who get pregnant out of wedlock are always expressing hostility toward their mothers, and occasionally both mother and father. This claim has not been supported by many of my counselees, although the desire to be loved often plays a significant role. However, the counseling pastor should be alert for hostility between mother and daughter. For this reason these girls are often reluctant to tell their parents when they have proof of their pregnancy. The minister should work toward a reconciliation with her parents, but sometimes this is not possible.

At this time of strong guilt feeling on the part of girl and boy, the pastor's understanding and acceptance will do much to alleviate the sense of separation from God. If the counselee desires to tell you about the experience, listen to her, but do not probe merely to satisfy your own curiosity. Do not err by giving hasty reassurance that God forgives her. Her own guilt must work its way out.

Special counseling sessions may be necessary with the parents of a girl or boy in such a situation, but this is not usually true in my experience. Parents have a way of being parents most of the time when their chicks are in trouble. Some are rigid, prideful and feel a sense of disgrace, but this is by far the exception to the rule. When confronted with such a situation take it slow and easy giving attention to the practical aspects of the situation and the emotional side of the problem will work itself out. Your own acceptance is the key to the situation.

I am sure no one can read this and the previous chapter and feel that the discussion has been adequate to supply all the needed information. My intention has been primarily to challenge you with the enormity of the task of pastoral care and counseling, and to set forth the boundary lines of opportunity and responsibility for the clergyman in his care of souls. You may feel that your interest and ability is in preaching, evangelism, and education. If so, your ministry in the local church is not that of a senior pastor. Someone else will surely inherit the role of the pastoral ministry that is rightfully your responsibility.

Some large churches are attempting to solve this problem by having a staff of people with diversified abilities. Theoretically, that division of labor should work. In point of fact, the members of large churches receive the poorest pastoral care. Rare is the minister who can be all things to all people. The demands upon his time are simply too great; his energies are drained, and he often loses heart. Even in our work as full-time professional counselors where we see one person at a time for a full hour, and where we are free of interruptions, we sometimes fail. Success is not guaranteed, not even for the professional counselor. The local pastor seldom has one uninterrupted hour with anyone. Yet, he must serve as: pastor, counselor, preacher, educator, administrator, evangelist, diplomat and protagonist, humorist and man of vision. His task is limited only by restrictions of time; opportunity and lack of specialized knowledge. Despite such handicaps, he provides the best he can in pastoral care to his people.

The specialized ministry is interesting. I have spent most of my life in it. But, the general pastoral task in the local church is far more important than the specialized ministry and we must seek to strengthen it.

FOUR

HEALTH and WHOLENESS

Negative Emotions (Destructive)	Positive Emotions (Healing-Redemptive)
Anxiety	Faith
Anger	Joy
Guilt Feelings	Forgiveness (Self Awareness)
Despair	Hope
Loneliness	Love
Pain	Courage
Boredom	Creative Work
Rejection	Acceptance

These two sets of emotions make us what we are.[1] The destructive emotions are not necessarily destructive, since without them it is doubtful if the human creature would long survive. The struggle to control and balance them inspires man to some of his noblest efforts. This is especially true in facing pain. While the destructive emotions are really symptoms of deeply-rooted problems, the symptoms themselves need priority consideration. The destructive emotions when out of control stir up trouble, while the healing-redemptive emotions endow life with meaning and purpose.

The pastor must be mindful of the full range of the emotional spectrum as he ministers in the home, hospital and office. The same concern will serve to revitalize his preaching and teaching ministry. The emotional equation cannot be dismissed as irrelevant in one's ministry to people. Harry Stack Sullivan, M.D., psychiatrist, has said, "We are the products of our interpersonal relations." The people

[1] See *Toward Health and Wholeness,* by Russell L. Dicks (New York, The Macmillan Company, 1960).

around us make us what we are; first our parents, our brothers and sisters; and later, our school companions, teachers, fellow students and professors, the men and officers in military service, the people with whom we work in business, industry and the professions. People, always people—their ideas, emotions, feelings, fears and anxieties, ambitions and hopes, loneliness and loves, rejections, frustrations, courage and acceptance—pour content and meaning into the crucible of our lives.

One's first cathedral of learning is the home. Here children learn their first lessons in tenderness or cruelty. Perhaps one should say tenderness *and* cruelty, for every home has some of both. Here also, the child is shuttled between alternating moods of harmony and discord; protective care and anxiety. The child experiences the conflict patterns between mother and father; he becomes an eyewitness to deceit, selfishness, harshness, and indifference. The more fortunate child is reared in the emotional climate of affection, courage, hope and joyfulness. One or the other of these emotional ranges will predominate, and this emotional preamble will strongly influence the child's life now and in the future. This is not to say that the pattern of life is hopelessly and irrevocably determined and set, despite the claims of behavioristic determinism.

People can and do change. "We are the products of our interpersonal relations." Our interpersonal relations are not the same 'twixt twelve and twenty as they were at age five or ten. Human emotions are never static. A single event may make a tremendous impact upon us. One person may touch and influence us with an emotional impact that becomes a part of us forever, particularly if the emotion between us was strong. We are a part of every person we have ever loved or hated and they are a part of us. We have a tendency to forget our hates, for hate is an illness and it is the nature of things, of the universe, of God to heal. There is healing power in the capacity to forget, and we strive to forget our hates. In actual fact we don't forget; it only appears that we do. Psychology teaches us that all meaningful experience is hidden in the recesses of our subconscious. Hate, while closely associated with love in many instances, may be strongly destructive and may seethe within as a destructive force for years.

Sharp anger which leaps into outbursts of temper is rooted in the same emotion. Some people cling to anger and hostility, unwilling to give it up lest they appear to be defaulting upon their rights as persons. This emotion is contrary to the deep nature of the universe. How do we know this to be true? How do we know it is not the intention of God and creation to destroy as well as to preserve, for in nature we see creature war upon creature? How do we know God is not neutral, perhaps indifferent to our needs and the needs of others around us?

This is a theological question and in one sense is beyond the scope of our discussion here; yet, in another sense it is a part of every pastoral situation confronting the pastor and his people. The pastor must have clear thoughts on the subject lest his own faith be weakened and he communicate doubt and uncertainty instead of hope. Without unconditional confidence in the healing nature of God, the minister becomes ineffectual.

My own convictions were not clear when I began my work in the hospital as a chaplain. There were many doubts and uncertainties to be resolved. During those early weeks and months of my hospital chaplaincy, little was expected of me. But, today, the pattern is different. A hospital chaplain is a member of the team selected to serve and to help sick people. He is no longer a learner, but a full partner. He is expected to provide positive help in the crises of life, not only in the hospital but in the other pastoral areas such as those described in Chapters 2 and 3. His base of operation, his justification for being, his professional anchor, his launching pad for flight into crises is his personal faith which undergirds and stabilizes the hope he communicates.

We are made for health, not sickness. As pastors, we share with God the crises in the lives of our people—the pastor helps to modulate these crises as acceptance struggles against rejection, as courage seeks to dominate pain, as hope disperses despair, as creativity replaces boredom, as joy drains away anger, as a sense of self awareness replaces guilt, as faith soothes anxiety, and as love enfolds loneliness. This transformation breaks into reality before our very eyes. The Lord's compassion comes as a healing leaven in the true pastoral ministry. We share these experiences with God for God is forever in the struggle.

Then what of failure? Where is God when fear predominates,

when hate persists, when pain, and loneliness, and boredom and despair destroy? We see this happen, too. Shall we conclude that God has failed? Or shall we view the failure as our own, or possibly a failure on the part of those others who stand in the background of tragedy: an alcoholic father long dead, an anxious fear-filled mother who depreciated marriage, an emotionally crippled jealousy-ridden older brother, a grandparent who lived in hatred rather than love, drawing away the life strength of their progeny and leaving them ill prepared for the pressures of living?

The human creature is made for health and functions with physical and emotional strength until the destructive emotions block the health-sustaining resources within him. Why one person becomes mentally ill and another physically ill we do not know. We are more interested here in health and wholeness than we are in illness. Operating from a belief that we are made for health the pastor confronted with a crisis in a parishioner must ask, what does the suffering mean? What lies back of this behavior? What does the crisis accomplish? What is a person working out?

A teen-ager rebelling against parental authority, running away from home, or failing in school, is trying to communicate something either to himself or his parents—perhaps to both. A woman trapped in a bad marriage develops a peptic ulcer and wonders why after years of conflict the ulcer now becomes active. The body has thus surrendered, and found this physical channel of release from emotional pressure. The body is made for health and functions in health until something intrudes to block the health process.[2]

"Thou shalt be happy" is not one of the Commandments, but neither is "Thou shalt be sick." In marriage we expect happiness. Yet, many who marry do not stop to consider what is happiness in marriage. Sometimes, unfortunately, marriages are entered with little thought except to get away from home, or to spite a former suitor. Our people expect happiness in life, and there is much to support this view both in the Old and New Testaments.

Jesus' new commandment is that a man first love God, and then his neighbor. Here, love is the keynote; not hate, not anxiety, not boredom, not loneliness. At the time the Ten Commandments were

[2] See Chapter 1, "The Healing Power of the Mind and Body," in *Toward Health and Wholeness,* op. cit.

given to the Israelites at Mt. Sinai, everyone had a God or Gods and knew it. Now, everybody has God, for without God in nature there could be no life, no orderliness, no creativity, but many do not know it. Modern man takes God very much for granted, neither understanding nor caring about the quality of the relationship. Let one fall ill or die, let marriage trouble come, let a severe personal crisis arise and then God becomes important. Then a person asks, "What of God?" in pleading or in anger and the minister must be prepared to answer the question although not often in words, for the suffering person cannot listen. Nevertheless, you must have an answer in your own mind lest you show your discomfort. Your words under such circumstances are not remembered but your poise, your confidence, your patience, your concern lives on. It is this spiritual stance that most often wins the patient's own battle against his doubt and anger.

The answer is, God is in the struggle, in the conflict, working through the healing redemptive emotions both within the suffering person and within the helping person. When they fail, God fails; when they succeed, God succeeds. We must be careful as to just when we assess an experience as failure for the failure of God may be in our own eyes, not in His. A person dying is with God; can that be tragic? A marriage breaking up may bring spiritual growth to one or both mates and relief from anxiety to children; is that bad? An alcoholic, long an immature and dependent person becomes mature and gains independence; is that not important? Life involves risks. It is not a sure thing that can be depended upon to act in the same responsible way at all times. It is filled with change, with newness, with adventure. We are made for health; we grow toward wholeness.

FIVE

WHY WE HELP PEOPLE

When people think of the clergyman they take it for granted that he is concerned about people in trouble; those who are sick, dying, grief suffering, hungry, discouraged. It never occurs to them to ask why he should be. The non-parishioner feels free to turn to the pastor for help as does the parishioner. Why should either expect him to help? Why is he considered a helping person? Why is anyone —doctor, nurse, social worker, trusted friends—concerned about helping people in trouble?

In this chapter we shall look at the *why* of helping people, recognizing that while compassion is a widespread reaction among people in general, the disciplined compassion of pastoral care is not something that is spontaneous.

Jesus said, "I give you a new commandment, that ye love one another." What was so new about it? Love in one form or another is as old as human existence. Love is the inclination to include others in the circle of one's concern. The initial concern is small at first and gradually increases in ratio to the involvement. All consciousness starts with self consciousness, self concern and self interest. The self is always at the center of the beginning stage. To accuse one of being selfish is to state the obvious; the act of unselfishness, of concern beyond one's self, of concern for another is the act of love.

The tiny baby is conscious only of itself and its own feelings of discomfort. The baby boy in the nursery does not cry because other babies around him are wet and hungry; he cries because *he* is wet and hungry. He stops crying when he gets attention for he learns within a few hours after birth that when he is picked up something nice happens to him. He has not yet identified his agent of relief but soon he will, and his gratitude, an incipient stage of love, will have started. As that experience is repeated over and over again, accompanied by caresses from soft warm hands with little pats and kisses and soft sounds of delight, the tiny baby is conditioned to love. The child's delight is not solely the reaction to mother love, although it usually is. Whatever the source of care and attention, there must be consistency and dependability. It is at this very point that we encounter the first snag in healthy living. Some mothers are not at all consistent and dependable. Uncertain, disorganized and insecure these are the mothers who fail in properly caring for their small baby, however helpless it is. They fail to give it food and warmth, clean diapers, and tender care with caresses and soft sounds.

While love is born, so also is frustration discovered and doubt planted. All grow, the good seed of love and affection together with the bad seeds of frustration and doubt. In some persons one of these outstrips the other; in some love grows into confidence and is strong; in some frustration and doubt develop into hate and anxiety, twin cousins which grow strong in their own right. All of these emotions are found in the average child and carry on their struggle to multiply. All *may* multiply, depending upon the life-given opportunities for each. Life advances through each successive stage of maturation. The struggle ferments within. The forces of strength, happiness, usefulness, and meaning interact with the opposing forces of sickness, uncertainty and frustration, drifting from goals and ideals to the point of self-destruction. Most lives have conflicting elements of each that are operative during short periods of time. The destructive patterns of uncertainty and sickness may pass quickly with help and good fortune. Without corrective measures, they may be prolonged. Some persons are predominantly one or the other throughout their lives, creative or destructive, healthy or sick, confident or uncertain, filled with love or hate.

"I give you a new commandment that ye love one another." Love, itself, within the close circle of family and friends was not a new concept. Jesus' application of God's commandment that men love and help one another beyond the close circle was new. That it was not then and has never been widely accepted is not so much a testimony against the validity of the commandment as it is a revelation of the failure of mothers and fathers, and substitute mothers and fathers, to find meaning for themselves and their children so that they can love. The search for *meaning* is basic in life. The new commandment—that ye love one another—and its fulfillment becomes meaning for the religious person. Whether Jesus was referring to love within the (Christian or Jewish) fellowship or all people everywhere makes little difference in our consideration here. If we are able to love, to be concerned, we will love beyond our own self and our own group. The question is, Why do we care? Why do we love? We love because love is *meaning;* caring is *meaning,* helping is *meaning.*

Why do doctors, nurses, pastors, social workers, and friends seek to help people? They help people because by helping people life takes on a new meaning. Helping one another is as old as human existence. With Jesus it took the form of a commandment—love God and love your neighbor; not just some neighbors, not just those that are like you. Is this command consistent with the nature of things? Is the human creature specially endowed with a natural capacity for love? "Nature is neither good nor bad," says Walt Disney as he presents his amazing films of the creatures of the field and desert, of the arctic north and tropical south. "Nature is neutral," he continues to say, and presents convincing evidence as we see creatures of the wild survive by destroying other creatures, only to be destroyed themselves by others. Watching a nature film gives one the strange feeling that one is experiencing a human drama of one person exploiting another only to be himself victimized by others.

A doctor spends twelve years in professional preparation. And, even with that vast treasury of knowledge, he may be only a mechanic, a highly skilled technician who is often incapable of affection for those who come through his office, his clinic and his operating room. One of the best surgeons in Chicago, a few years ago, had difficulty talking to people. One of the busiest psychiatrists of a large city is hard working and ambitious. Yet, he is cold, awkward and disliked by most of his patients because they feel uncomfortable in his presence. Many social workers give the impression no one has a right to help people unless he has a master's degree in social work. But, why do social workers seek to help people? Why do surgeons, psychiatrists, and pastors proffer their services to those who are sick and in trouble?

A few years ago, the pastor of a large church in Cleveland said,

"Pastoral counseling is a fad that will soon pass." My response upon hearing this statement was to ask, "Is it a fad to die?" To this question one could add, "Is it a fad to be lonely, to be sad, to suffer from whatever cause?" If so, then it is a fad to try to help people and it is a fad to care whether suffering people are helped or not. Large amounts of our tax money and much of our charitable giving is for purposes of alleviating suffering of all kinds: hospitals, children's homes, welfare and research. We give because we or our loved ones may benefit directly or indirectly. We identify ourselves with the man in needy circumstances because we ourselves have been there, or fear that we some day may suffer a similar fate. It was a nurse whose name and face I have long since forgotten who linked her fingers into my hair and lifted my head, turning it so that I would not strangle in my own vomitus following an operation. When I tried to apologize for the unpleasantness of the task, she was embarrassed saying it was her job.

As we fall asleep before surgery we sense that we are completely helpless. Yet, we trust those who will care for us. The surgical staff and nurses do not love us for they scarcely know us. They may by nature have little of the spirit of generosity. They may neither know nor care that a Nazarene living nearly two thousand years ago in a remote part of the world, whose dress and speech and manner would be completely strange to them, said, "I command that you love one another. It is a must." And yet they function, as members of the helping arts of our time, to our benefit. We express our gratitude and remunerate them to the best of our ability. Yet, the least intricate of their operations is actually more expensive than the patient undergoing surgery could afford. Thus, most of us carry insurance, pay taxes, and contribute to health and community appeal drives. Each person involved in the construction and maintenance of a hospital from the bricklayer who erects the physical plant, the secretary filling out Blue Cross records, the engineer who maintains the building to the surgeon who performs the operation finds a very special meaning for their lives in helping to meet the needs of others.

We are ministers. We know the authority and meaning of the words, "Love ye one another." We believe they are pivotal for our ministry; we believe they are the essence of the good news for all mankind. Over and over again Jesus lived them, demonstrated them, personalized them, gave them flesh and bones and breathed life into them. How, then, could they have failed so badly these many years? Failed? We have welfare and hospitals with thousands of people working at the job of helping people. We give millions of dollars to help the underdeveloped nations, people less fortunate than ourselves. Formerly, we gave through voluntary effort. Today, much of our giving is through government channels with government direction. Now the government dictates our giving to suffering people.

The minister serving the local church is supported by those he serves. How he ministers when he comes to you during illness, when your son is arrested for breaking street lights, when your daughter becomes pregnant out of wedlock, when you hate your son-in-law, when your mother does more to help your brother than you, or in many other similar instances will have little direct relationship to the way he earns his living, his ordination vows, or even his academic achievements. His helpfulness will rather depend upon the dimension of his love for people; and upon the spectrum of his perception of human need as the lessons of life have opened those vistas to him.

Dr. Leslie Hohman, psychiatrist, used to say, "The good counselor is one who has wisdom." I once pressed him to define wisdom. According to Dr. Hohman, the wise counselor must have common sense, to be able to give explanations in simple terms, permit a person to make his own decisions, avoid giving a mass of moralizing cant, be willing to stand against community prejudices, have a compassionate attitude, have a knowledge of what he can do so far as skill is concerned, and know that people who seek his help do not need *the* decision as much as they need *a* decision.

Dr. Hohman has been a psychiatrist thirty-five years, first at Johns Hopkins Hospital where he was the resident of Dr. Adolph Meyer, the father of American psychiatry, and later at Duke Medical Center. He has served both as a physician and a teacher of physicians. It is interesting to note that his description of wisdom applies to both pastoral counselor and physician. He does not use the word love, but speaks rather of "compassionate attitude." He expects the counselor to be courageous. Just how the counselor is to achieve these virtues or *why* Dr. Hohman does not say; the why would be related to one's motivation for wanting to be a doctor or minister.

It is easy to say that we seek to serve people because our Lord has commanded it. In the final analysis that *is* the real reason. However, even without his command we would have reached the same conclusion as we studied the life and teachings of our Lord for it stands at the very heart of the gospel. It is just as deeply rooted in the heart of Judaism as Christianity. It is in other religions, also.

Pastoral care for each minister is a slowly evolving, tedious, highly personal subject that becomes meaningful as he walks, talks, waits, prays, gives and receives love from someone touched by tragedy. Then it is more than an academic subject. It is only of limited help to you to read case histories and study the techniques of someone else engaged in counseling, just as the medical student studying another doctor's diagnosis is largely untouched by the exercise. But as limited as such an approach may be, there are benefits to be derived from it by the inexperienced. Counseling becomes meaningful when you are involved. We can study "relationships" objectively. We can study love. We can study both the negative (dislike) and positive (like) relationship. We can study both our own and others. Just as the astronauts study their performance charts and reactions after an orbital flight—so also can we study the helping process. So we can study how we helped when we did and why we failed when we failed. But as we study we must realize it is still an academic exercise that will become meaningful as we ourselves become involved in the actual task of helping people.

In the past, ministers have spoken of themselves as being "called to preach." Observing many of those who have been most certain of this call and seeing how complete is their failure in fulfilling "the new commandment" one is somewhat skeptical of the validity of the call of many. So far, we have made little progress in evaluating and testing the minister's capacity to care for people, to give and receive love. Perhaps such a test is even now being devised. There is little doubt that such capacity varies from time to time within a given person. Our needs to give compassion are limited by changing circumstances at a given moment of time.

A doctor or minister is often belittled by others because of failures within his own life. These failures may be the very foundation upon which his effectiveness turns. George Truett, the great Baptist preacher of Dallas, Texas, once killed a man in a hunting accident. How much the heartache he felt from this tragedy contributed to his concern for people cannot be known. Because a psychologist's own boy has been in trouble does not make him ineffective as a counselor for parents; perhaps just the opposite.

One thing is certain in regard to the subject of "Why We Care" as it relates to pastors and other professional helping people. It is this. When you come to die, the thing that will be important is not the number of mistakes you have made, or even the use or abuse of your talents. The really important consideration that will give you comfort will be the affection that you have given and received.

I give you a commandment, love ye one another. Here is a royal edict, a Divine proclamation. We care because we cannot, dare not, pull around to bypass a man lying in the road; we cannot stand to see people, the people of God, die. "Inasmuch as ye have done it unto the least of these, ye have done it unto me." When gave we them a cup of water? We were so busy caring for them we did not even know we were doing it for it was life itself to us.

Erich Fromm, a psychologist, remarked upon the occasion of the seventy-fifth birthday of Paul Tillich, a theologian, "Modern man is lonely, frightened and hardly capable of love. He wants to be close to his neighbor, and yet he is too unrelated and distant to be close."

Man's need for love is second only to his need for food and at times even hunger is set aside for love. Love begins with gratitude and moves forward through acceptance to understanding. Jesus said, "Love God and love your neighbor as you love yourself." For love to be free flowing and generous one must not have self hatred.

Human relations are primary for the Jew. Love of fellow creature is obedience to the Law. Man's delight is in the Law; his joy is in studying it; absorbing and being absorbed into it; in following it and being supported by God as he follows it. Thus he finds contentment and meaning for his life. The Law constantly directs that man shall be concerned about his neighbor. He is directed to give succor to the needy, comfort to the sorrowing and affection to the lonely. "Love ye one another" is a commandment to both Jew and Christian.

The church has been described as "the fellowship of the concerned"; but concerned about what and for whom? As we said earlier, all concern starts with the self and then broadens to include others, others who are within our close family circle. In fact, without a good family relationship, it is difficult although not impossible to expand this concern. If our early experiences are satisfying and the hurts are minimal, then our concern expands readily. A former divinity student of mine who understood himself fairly well used to respond to skeptical undergraduate students in his dormitory, when in "bull sessions" they questioned the existence of God. Before engaging in any discussion on this subject, he would challenge them by saying, "Tell me first of your feelings toward your old man." Always, he reported, those who claimed they did not believe in God admitted they had bad feelings toward their fathers. The commandment, "Honor thy father and thy mother" is lost upon those who have felt rejection by parents unless help can be secured to overcome these negative feelings and replace them with feelings of understanding and acceptance.

The church is not a fellowship of saints. It is a group of imperfect people who are concerned about themselves and as they mature, if they do, with their fellow creatures. Jesus said, in effect, "I came not to the well but the sick, not to the content but to the downhearted, not to the perfect but the imperfect, not the saint but the sinner." This almost makes one want to be sick, downhearted, imperfect, a sinner, in order to have fellowship with him, to feel his nearness and his affection, doesn't it? Well . . . who did we say was perfect? The message of love is for all people, not just those in trouble at the moment.

Not always is the troubled soul accessible for help. Some refuse help, some are unable to accept help, some live in such a world of chaos, doubt, distrust, hurt, that they cannot accept. Their ears are closed, their senses blunted. There is no trust within them, no generosity, only fear or hate, sometimes fear *and* hate.

The church is a group of people in love with the central figure of the Christian Church, Jesus Christ; as that love becomes strong they are able to love one another. As they understand him and the love that flows into them from him, they reach out to others; just as the love two people feel for each other overflows into the lives of others through the joyfulness of their affection. So the joyfulness of the love of God overflows to others. As pastors, we start with joy and move to concern and through concern to joy again. Sometimes we fail, and of these failures we must be self-critical and resolved to move toward self improvement.

In a sense, pastoral failure and the failure of the fellowship of the concerned is a re-enactment of the crucifixion. A common expression is, "We preach Jesus Christ and Him crucified." His birth and death, traditional theologians would say, is a sign of the revelation of God's love for the world. If Jesus is preached as crucified only then nothing has happened beyond the death of a good man. If Jesus is resurrected, then victory is gained inasmuch as love has triumphed over fear and hate. Jesus personified love; his concern for the suffering person was the concern of love for those who are hurt and not hurt in whatever state. Love was killed—crucified—by the forces of anxiety and hate. Love was destroyed, and with that destruction a mood of discouragement overtook his followers. This happens to pastors and laymen, alike, when they see love fall.

In the resurrection, love lives again and his followers take heart; they become strong to move into the world "changed men" for now they move with courage. Jesus wept for the suffering of the world but not for long. Soon, his joy returned. We grieve for our own loneliness in the death and separation from a loved one. Our grief is not the death of love but the separation from love. Even in the moments of bereavement, love continues for love does not die whether it be love of person or love of God. Sadness comes to us, yes, but love is forever resurrected. Love lives. We love or we perish, as Dr. Smiley Blanton has said, in his book by that title.[1]

We seek to help people because we are forever re-enacting the love we know through Christ. The re-enactment is imperfect because we are imperfect. If we become preoccupied with the imperfection, we may fail completely. It is sad to love and fail. Far worse than that is the life in which there is no love at all.

Some may say I confuse the love of God (Agape) with the love of man (Eros). It seems to me these two love experiences are always

[1] *Love or Perish*, Revised Edition (New York, Simon and Schuster, Inc. 1957).

intertwined. We love God because we have felt human love of family and friends; we love our fellow human creatures because God loves us and created love within us. He created us imperfect that we may share the joy of creative love with him. We fail, he fails, but love forever tries again. Therein lies hope.

SIX

The RELATIONSHIP of PASTORAL CARE to the CHURCH

Pastoral care is an integral part of the task of the church. It represents the believer's concern for the recurring needs of one's fellow man. The church's concern embraces such diversified activities as premarital guidance, care of the dying, support of world missions, fund raising, religious instruction, maintenance of grounds and equipment, boy scout troops, altar guild activities, recreation, hospital visitation and social action in community, state and nation. Some program of pastoral care is carried on in every church whether large or small; city, suburban or rural; liturgical or informal. The question does not center upon whether or not such a program will be initiated. The question relates rather to the quality and effectiveness of the program. Thus, the big question is: "Are we really helping people in their times of greatest need?"

Resistance

Twofold resistance has delayed the progress of pastoral care. The first point of resistance involves vocabulary. Part of the vocabulary of the new pastoral care has been adopted from medicine and psychiatry, both equally difficult; an additional part from social work which is even more vague; and still more terms are derived from psychology which shifts so rapidly that psychologists themselves cannot keep abreast of the pace. Finally, we have contributed our own vocabulary. Some of this resistance has come from clergy who, as a British surgeon once said, "I'm getting to that age where anything new makes me mad." Almost every instructor with training in clinical pastoral education who has served upon a theological faculty has been viewed with alarm by his confreres. When I was appointed to one theological faculty a colleague expressed his concern at a faculty meeting: "Does this mean we are becoming a trade school?" He had not bothered to inquire into the content of my courses. He was simply disturbed by change and the unfamiliar. Later, he modified his views, but never felt quite comfortable when pastoral care was discussed for, basically, he was an insecure person. Professors of the older disciplines have accepted the need to teach seminarians how to preach wisely, recognizing the practical need for such instruction. Yet, the same recognition has not been accorded to the importance of pastoral care through counseling. There remains the haunting fear that modern psychiatry is a humanistic philosophy which threatens to weaken one's total ministry.

We are always threatened by what we do not understand. In Chapter Five, we spoke of helping people because of the love of God which finds its way into our hearts. It might seem that love of God alone is not sufficient to understand why we accept and love people. A theological faculty member of my acquaintance committed suicide. This was, indeed, a heartbreaking tragedy. But, even more tragic was the reaction of a faculty associate who raised the question as to whether the funeral should be held in the chapel, because the death had been self-inflicted.

The second point of resistance involves the balance of program and activities to allow adequate time for pastoral care whether within the parish or beyond its immediate bounds. This has led inevitably to the questioning of the church's program and the content of its preaching. Tradition dies a hard death. When established parish practices are examined and challenged, moans, groans and loud noises are heard. Abraham Lincoln, in his second annual address, said, "The dogmas of the quiet past are inadequate to the stormy present. As our case is new, so we must think anew. We must disenthral ourselves, and then we shall save our country." I am sure that Dr. Boisen in his work at the Worcester State Hospital, and I in mine at the Massachusetts General Hospital, had no thought of *disenthralling* ourselves from the church. Rather, we considered our work to be an extension of the church even though our hospitals had no organic relationship with organized religion. However, it is significant to note that it was at the instigation of two physicians that a clergyman sent out the first letter to the citizens of Boston in 1809 that led to the founding of the Massachusetts General Hospital. This letter stated in part, "We desire to found a hospital for the care of idiots and other patients." The mentally ill were then classified as idiots.

Many of the clergy who have since gone into the specialized ministry of pastoral counseling and pastoral care have done so to *disenthral* themselves from the tediousness of church program. Some have rightly recognized that they had little talent for preaching and parish administration. Nevertheless, they felt called to serve as ministers out of a strong love for God and people and have accepted positions as chaplains. Other fields await further exploration and description.[1] As the description of the field of pastoral care advanced, the enormity of the task became apparent. Clergy were challenged in an ever increasing way to do a more adequate job. The area of pastoral care with which I was involved—a ministry to the sick and dying—did not meet with the same resistance as did the pastoral care for the mentally sick and emotionally disturbed. This resistance is still evident, and with some good reason. The local pastor simply does not have the time to devote twenty to fifty hours with one emotionally disturbed person even if he has had adequate training to guide him. Nor does he have the time and energy to work with many troubled marriages when the needed time for counseling may range from eight to twenty or more hours. Resistance in the church to the new pastoral care is directed more at the concept of the minister's formal counseling, than it is toward hospital and home calling, especially in those instances where he spends his time seeing non-parishioners.

I am convinced that in spite of our inclination to *disenthral* ourselves from program and preaching, the local pastor seeking to be all things to all people has the greatest opportunity to help people. The minister stands at the frontier of human emotions. Generally speaking, he is the first person contacted by those who most need pastoral help. His ability to provide pastoral care and to refer where

[1] See Appendix A, *New Frontiers of Pastoral Care.*

deeper professional insights are needed are tremendous assets to those in need.

The poorest job of such contacts is in the big church with memberships of a thousand or more. There the pastoral task becomes almost impossible.

Many of America's larger churches are moving in the direction of employing clinically trained counselors. It is still too early to predict what percentage of these efforts will succeed. The senior pastor of one such church told me of his experience with a specialized counseling program, "It does not pay its way." There was no word of appreciation of the work done—only "it does not pay." What he meant by his use of the word "pay" was that the counselor's work did not return sufficient cash into the church's treasury to pay the additional salary. This was a poor standard of evaluation.

The success or failure of such an effort sometimes depends upon the way the counseling pastor is introduced to the congregation as well as the continuing educational effort to interpret counseling. It is important that one avoid giving the impression that counseling deals with "screwballs." Every pastor on the staff should be available for counseling and should be trained to do counseling. It will be a long time, however, before this is true. The pendulum need not swing so far that the minister without counseling talent will feel he has no place in the service of the church any more than one who has little or no talent in the pulpit should feel he has no place in the ministry.

It seems perfectly obvious that pastoral care, the concern for people, the "love one another" stands at the heart of the church. Without it the church dies. Ministry to individuals—the one to one relationship—is the place where deeper concern is realized in a way that is not possible in the service of public worship. In worship, one may feel close to God, but not to persons. This same acceptance may be gained in small working groups within the church where affection and a sense of belonging becomes personalized. This, too, is pastoral care.

Rejection

There are people who have been through certain crises and suffering toward whom the church (pastors and parishioners) have trouble communicating acceptance. All too often, the only thing these sufferers have in common with the church is the same old pattern of rejection. Such is the fate of the divorced person, the alcoholic, the person who has tried to commit suicide, and the homosexual. Nor does the mentally ill person completely escape the wide berth given him by many church people. "You need to see a psychiatrist" are fighting words to many. Recently, a woman sat in my office weeping at the suggestion that she see a psychiatrist. Whereupon, she replied, "I can't do that to my son." Only a few years ago the T.B. patient suffered under this same sense of social stigma.

We are threatened by that which we do not understand and by what we cannot control. In our efforts to help people, we seek to conform to the set standards of behavior. In effect, we say, "Be like us." This is not love. The hidden compulsion to help people is selfishness at a deep level. "He that would save his life shall lose it," according to Jesus. Paradoxical as it seems, it works. Become interested in someone, take time with him, and listen to him as he searches for meaning. Soon you will be calling him friend, praying for him when he is in difficulty, suffering with him in times of anguish.

"I don't know who you (as a minister) are interested in but there is a woman whom I think needs to see a minister," a social worker said. "I guess I need to see a minister," a man said who was trapped in the deep shadows of grief. "I know the doctor can do only so much and the patient must do the rest and I'm afraid I can't do my part," a woman explained to the minister on the eve of her operation. Why? Why do these and many others turn to pastors? They do so because of a recognized need for courage, faith, hope, and acceptance. From time immemorial, the church has sustained such a ministry. Will it continue to do so? How shall we ministers respond to the alcoholic, the mentally ill, the dying? Are we threatened by the person who has tried to commit suicide because we ourselves have one time contemplated suicide? Are we uncomfortable because we ourselves have wanted a divorce, or know that our spouses have entertained the thought? Is divorce a sin? What, then, is sin?

Consider anew, the Parable of the Talents. What happened to the man who buried his talent? Marriage may destroy talent, alcohol may destroy talent, suicide may destroy talent and worry may destroy talent; for cruelty and hate and worry and discouragement destroy love. Whatever destroys love is sin.

Many ministers and lay leaders in the church have made bitter pronouncements against divorce, and then wondered why people with marital difficulty have shunned the church. The fact that a couple has not resorted to divorce has become one of the standards by which we have judged goodness and marital success. Yet, we have ignored the loveless condition in many homes. It has already been indicated that seventy per cent of the teen-agers seen in our counseling center last year were emotionally insecure youngsters living in homes where the marriage was intact.

The church sat out the growing problem of alcoholism, although it was a churchman, Bishop James Cannon of Virginia, who prepared the amendment upon prohibition. Following the failure and repeal of the eighteenth amendment, church leaders largely withdrew from their campaign against alcoholism. When psychiatry and medicine publicly referred to alcoholism as a disease, the church continued to maintain an evasive silence. Such inaction is understandable. Church leaders had few significant insights into the problem; they simply did not understand it. How a person can day after day, time after time, do that which he "would not and not do that which he would," moving ever closer to death, hurting those he holds most dear, is simply not comprehensible to anyone not closely involved with the problem.

Mr. James Oughton, director of the Keeley Institute in Dwight, Illinois, scores the medical doctor's attitude toward the problem, "The doctor is a scientist until he faces someone with the alcohol problem. Then he becomes a moralist." One doctor told me, "The alcoholic has the capacity to trigger more hostility in me than any other person." When doctors trained to treat disease feel this way, it is understandable why church people reject alcoholics. We dislike that which we cannot control.

Mental depression is an illness. One of its symptoms is the desire to commit suicide. Like most other diseases there are degrees in the severity of the illness. Accordingly, some depressed people think more seriously about suicide than others. Suicide now ranks tenth on the listing of causes of death in the United States.

In the eyes of the church, suicide is defiance of God. The rejection of living is a rejection of the life that God has given. For some it is the rejection of suffering, either physical pain or mental anguish. Suffering, too, may be said to be a free gift; whether from God's perfection or imperfection is not for our consideration here. Suffering always brings with it the opportunity for growth and creativity. The suicide rejects this new birthright spawned in suffering. Deeply recessed within most of us is the fear of those who attempt self-destruction, lest the same inclination engulf us. Because of the risk to self, we feel we dare not be friendly (accepting) with such a person. A woman told me, "I will commit suicide some day because my husband did and I loved him." She probably will not unless she becomes depressed, and then she may.

Self-assurance in counseling those prone to suicide rests upon our own basic health. We have previously observed that the forces of health are pitted against the forces of illness within us and in the community around us; in our family circle, school, factory, town, state, nation, and world society. If all is not well *in* mother or father, *between* mother and father, in brother or sister, between students and faculty, labor and management, the governor and his cabinet, the president and congress; if there is trouble in the Congo, starvation in Japan, epidemic in Finland, it affects us. Suicide, personal or national, is a threat. We do not handle a threat by ignoring it or by magic incantations. We accept it, seek to understand it, and then venture forth to divest it of controlling power.

Homosexuality, like most sexual aberrations, is shrouded in mystery, shame and embarrassment. Until recently the word could not be mentioned in polite society. Small wonder, then, that little progress has been made in understanding the homosexual. It is not yet decided whether homosexuality is a disease or a way of life, but in either case we are threatened by it. In time it will be understood calmly. Even so, the perpetuation of the race is not seriously endangered by the practice.

The altar before which we worship God is sufficient to overcome our feelings of insecurity and our inclinations to reject those whose behavior, color, even way of life is different from our own. At the close of World War I a company of French soldiers moved into a German village in the Ruhr during the occupation. Tension quickly mounted between the French soldiers and the German villagers. This tension reached its peak of hatred between the French captain and the German mayor until all wondered if open violence could be avoided. On Christmas Eve the villagers and French soldiers made their way to the only church in the area for communion. Suddenly, a deep quiet fell over the church as the German mayor and the French captain were observed to be making their way to the altar from different parts of the church. The worshipers stepped back as the two enemies knelt for communion. They were no longer enemies, but worshipers before the altar of God, the Almighty. In the days that followed, tension slackened and the occupation moved forward to its conclusion.

The church at its best is made up of people seeking to find new meaning in life for themselves and their children. With each new discovery of God's love for us, comes the growth in capacity to accept our fellow man, no matter what his state or condition. Brotherhood is set into action, and the power of love begins its healing process—through us.

PART TWO

PRACTICES

SEVEN

HOW WE HELP PEOPLE

The story is told that when Ernest Fremont Tittle, for many years the great prophetic voice in the Middle West, went as a young minister to the First Methodist Church, Evanston, Illinois he spoke out upon social and economic problems. After a few months of such leadership, prominent members of the congregation decided together to petition the Bishop to move Dr. Tittle at the next Annual Conference. The success of this strategy pivoted on the active support of one outstanding layman. When the committee approached him for support, they were amazed by his reaction. He said, "All of you know my views. I don't agree with everything Tittle is saying on social and economic issues, but when my wife died that young preacher came and sat up with me all night. He can preach in that pulpit and say anything he wants to as long as he wants to and I'll back his right to say it." The committee did not call upon the Bishop.

Henry Sloan Coffin, former President of Union Theological Seminary, New York and long-time pastor of the Madison Avenue Presbyterian Church, wisely counseled his students, "Hold back your controversial sermons until your people have gotten to know you and until you've been in their homes, then they will listen to you."

Dr. Tittle's experience and Dr. Coffin's advice point to a basic principle in helping people: know and love them and you will help them spiritually, emotionally and intellectually. People we like can help us; people we dislike hurt us.

The words of Jesus are clear on this point, "I give you a new commandment, that ye love one another." Pastorally, help comes through rapport, a positive interpersonal relationship, a feeling of trust, of understanding, of acceptance, of affection. The Roman Catholic Church with the wisdom of centuries speaks of "Mother Church," and addresses its clergy as "Father." Now, psychology has helped us understand that the helping person is more a mother figure than father—that the pastor must have the sensitivity of mother with the objectivity of father. Although the mother protects her child, she knows instinctively that he must become an adult. Over-protection does not help and almost always hurts. Making another's decision delays the maturing process.

The child will by nature cling to parental protection. His world is immense, and filled with unknown terrors. But, as he matures, the child ventures farther and farther out on his own. He cannot keep from it for he is pushed from within toward new experience. These natural inclinations are colored by the attitudes, the courage, the anxieties, the confidence, the relationship he sees and feels around him, in mother, in father, in big brother and sister, in the boy next door and the girl down the street; and now—by that monster or benefactor, we still do not know which it is but we suspect it is both—the *television*. Here adventure touches the child's imagination, his sense of humor, his desire to participate. It is his nature to grow, and he will grow either in a healthy self-confident way, or if anger and anxiety and hurt fill his home, if tears and screams, threats and abuse surround him, he may withdraw and never venture far. A child may be emotionally crippled at a young age, but most are not; he may be hurt but not seriously handicapped, for healing is deep in the heart of the universe.

Children survive their parents' anxieties and come to adulthood, at various ages, and under various conditions and for various reasons they are confronted by a pastor. They have talked to him as teenagers about their choice of a life work or a life mate; they have met him in their homes and in church and Sunday School; they have felt his influence as he comes to the home or hospital in time of grief, or family crisis. They have sat with him to plan their wedding and listened to his counsel about marriage and family living. They have been inspired and bored and instructed by his words in sermons and prayers and conversations. And then one day a pastor, perhaps a different man entirely, for the minister of one's youth may have relocated in another church, finds his way to us or we to him as we seek or welcome his help.

Seward Hiltner has talked of "precounseling influence." Others have spoken of "the image of the pastor" which the parishioner has in his mind at the outset of pastoral conversation. A man and wife had quarrelled all night. Early the next morning they stormed into the county courthouse to petition for an immediate divorce. They wanted the nasty mess untangled by 10 A.M. The courthouse clerk sent them directly to me. Fortunately, my schedule was such that I could see them immediately. I quickly learned that they were members of a church that frowns upon divorce.

After his anger subsided and the husband became comfortable in our conversation he remarked, "It's a cinch I didn't want to talk to any damn preacher." Two interviews later when he discovered I was a minister, he apologized. His image of a minister was that of a person who would object to his views with censure and moralizations. Actually, the marriage was salvaged. It would have shattered had the husband been called upon to face more criticism. He had already had an overdose of criticism from his wife, mother, and well-intentioned friends. Every pastor's reception in a home or in a crisis situation is influenced by the pastoral image a counselee has in his mind at the outset of the conversation. This image or stereotype can readily change in the mind of the counselee. Much will depend upon his reaction to you as the counselor. The old image may reappear if you touch tender spots or if anxiety-producing ideas come up. On the other hand, reassurance may be communicated in innumerable ways. You are always reminding people who accept you of a beloved cousin or uncle or friend.

Dr. Sam Howie of Oak Ridge, Tennessee, says the chief role of the minister in the pulpit is to demonstrate the kind of person he is so that people will know whether they can talk to him about personal problems. If he speaks out strongly against divorce and credits it with being responsible for the high delinquency rate, persons who have been divorced will not come to him with other problems; if he attacks alcohol and drinking, the alcoholic or near-alcoholic will avoid him; if he berates the morals of young people and associates dancing with immorality, parents who approve of dancing will not talk to him about children who are having difficulty. "I say to you, love one another." Can we love those with whom we disagree? What is more important, can they love us? Can they accept the help we have to offer when we have angered them? Does our preaching strengthen the healing-redemptive emotions in our people or does it stir the destructive emotions? Worse still, does it do neither—no hits, no runs, no errors?

Much could be written about today's negative preaching. Actually, negative preaching is easier, for we as preachers and parishioners struggle at the point of pain and discontent. One's consciousness is sharpest there. Dr. Harry Emerson Fosdick used to tell his students about the book of theology which he studied as a student. The first chapter was entitled, "Hell" and the second, "Hell Continued." Such was the theological outlook early in the century—hell and more hell, suffering and more suffering. This continues to be the message of some—suffering and more suffering. The fact of suffering is still quite as real as early in the century although the type has shifted. In those days, the emphasis was upon physical pain and hunger; today the base has shifted to anxiety, anger and frustration. A generation ago, man was concerned with his physical survival. He still is, but to that he has added discontentment as well. Man, today, has more material possessions than any previous generation in history. Despite his abundance, he lacks security.

If your personal concept of a valid ministry centers upon hell and more hell, rejection and more rejection, avoid counseling. Do not presume to minister pastorally to the sick, the dying, the grief suffering, the sad, the lonely, the indisposed in spirit. Do not attempt to grapple with those caught in despair. Nor should you seek out the anxiety sufferer, the angry and lonely. If they know your views on such matters, it is certain they will not seek you out. Can you preach of heaven without hell? Can you think of hope without despair? Can you be creative without first being bored? If not, then what of immortality? One woman asked a cruel and vindictive husband, "Can't you ever be happy?" He replied, "I would be miserable if I were happy." So was his mother before him, the wife reported.

We help people only when we have a genuine concern. We see them not as miserable sinners who are "unsaved," but as people—sons and daughters of God who are our brethren. We do not instantaneously love them, but we do shown concern. Love develops much along the lines of our previous discussion in Chapter 5. This relationship develops in proportion to the person's need for help and our capacity to respond to that need. Our capacity to help is limited only by our compassion, skill and available time. If we have the know-how, skill, concern, and sufficient time, there is no person, theoretically, that we cannot help in some significant way. This is true whether we be ministering to the dying person, the alcoholic, the grief suffering or the homosexual. Periodically, we find it necessary to re-examine our goals for they vary with the situation and the person.

It would appear that the goal in marriage counseling would always be reconciliation and the rebuilding of the marriage. Especially is this so in marriages where there are children. Yet, a word of caution is in order. Children suffer daily hurts in homes where there is conflict. Unless marital discord can be resolved and replaced with tenderness and affection, the children continue to suffer.

The records in our marriage counseling files are filled with examples of marriage where the choice was made to live in a destructive marriage rather than seek divorce. Now we, as counselors, deal with the recurring upheavals of those marriages. Here is an example. An attractive thirty-year-old woman, mother of two children, reports a childhood home of conflict in which her father worked spasmodically, drank heavily, constantly abused her mother and chased after other women. Her hard-working mother preferred even this marriage to divorce. Of three children, one brother became an alcoholic, a sister has gone through two divorces while my counselee is now undecided about the future of her own marriage. She is unable to give or receive affection. While she yearns for love, her feelings are dead for she cannot believe in anyone, herself included. She is of the decided opinion that her mother's decision to stay married to her father emotionally handicapped each of the children. Those scars mark her own children who now live in a home where parental affection is neither seen nor felt.

The goal in ministering to the sick is to deal with whatever destructive emotions are there. The doctor will give his primary attention to the alleviation of physical pain. When pain is prolonged, it becomes a religious and philosophical problem. The patient will frequently raise serious questions about the nature and sovereignty of God when pain is sharp and persistent. The doctor is ill prepared to deal with the religious and philosophical aspects of pain.

The goal of the pastor in ministering to the dying is to deal with guilt feelings, loneliness and regret and to support and strengthen faith so that the patient dies with courage strong and dignity intact looking forward with hope and not backward with regret. When the mother of William and Henry James of Cambridge, Massachusetts, died, the family had a celebration, saying, "Mother has now moved into that which she has so long anticipated." And so the teeth of grief are pulled even before a death. Still, grief remains. Our tears of grief flow from our loneliness and separation, rather than from despair for the spiritual welfare of the departed. Here we can but trust the compassion of God.

Our goal in ministering to senior citizens is to deal with the corroding influence of loneliness and help give time meaning. Our goal in evangelistic calling is to establish contact and invite the individual or family into the church fellowship. One displays poor judgment in interjecting testimony into the conversation or by arguing doctrine. If serious questions are raised, brief explanations should certainly be given. Where crises situations are evident in evangelistic calling, these should be dealt with as in routine calling.

The goal in routine calling is to establish or strengthen the relationship. Specific techniques will be described in the next chapter. In a sense, the routine call of the pastor is similar to the routine physical examination by the physician. The pastoral methods are less dependable and the working data less exact. The completeness of a medical examination will depend upon what tests the doctor wishes to make. Such tests will not be identical for each patient. Nevertheless, there will be an evident similarity in procedure. A similar situation applies to the pastor in his routine call. His accomplishments are likely to be limited by the duration of the call and the number of calls he can make. Little can be accomplished in a call of less than thirty minutes. Routine calls and those made to senior citizens are the ones most likely to be neglected once the minister increases his counseling sessions.

The pastor's goals with the alcoholic are sobriety and a healthy life. Sometimes complete sobriety cannot be gained. Leslie R. Hohman, M.D. and psychiatrist, has frequently urged ministers not to be discouraged if the drinking periods are lessened, but a person still has an occasional relapse. The goal in working with the relatives of an alcoholic may be supportive. In such instances, the mate's resentment may be lessened and her self-confidence strengthened, or it may be to make a major decision, such as seeking a divorce.

The goal of working with the pregnant girl out of wedlock is to help her and her family to formulate a plan of action, and to restore the girl's self-confidence. It is generally necessary to help the family to accept the awkward situation, and to creatively meet their sense of guilt and parental failure.

It is evident that pastoral goals vary. Some are specific; some are vague or somewhat nebulous; some are superficial, some have depth. Some goals can be achieved rather quickly and with relative ease; others are involved and never fully realized. The anxiety sufferer, for example, continues in anxiety, since he never really achieves the contentment he says he seeks. Perhaps he really does not want contentment, but only thinks he does. Even though the pastor refers the counselee for psychiatric treatment and he receives psychotherapy, there still remains a pastoral relationship.

The pastor helps people by his own spiritual stance. His courage begets courage. His faith in God and the meaningfulness in life inspires others. He helps through his judgment much in the manner described by Robert Browning, "God teaches us to help each other, lending out our minds." In crises situations one loses his perspective and depends upon a trusted pastor (friend) for guidance. With understanding and wisdom, the pastor helps people directly, or refers them to others who may have greater professional skill in a given area. Where emotional tension upset and disturb the individual, the pastor should prove to be the most beneficial source of help.

To understand how the pastor helps people, one must under stand the actual relationship that exists between parishioner and pastor. It is through this relationship that hope, faith, concern, judgment, courage, joy is communicated.

Rapport, a word borrowed from the French psychiatric literature, was originally called *en rapport.* The root meaning is trust, friendliness, affection. By definition, the word is positive. The casual student is inclined to underestimate its meaning and significance in human relationships. Actually, the roots go deep, and the branches reach widely. When I was a student in a mental hospital, the term was first introduced to our class. We used it with great flourish until one day a rare experience gave it special meaning. You might say I backed into an understanding of rapport. Each trainee was assigned one or two patients for study and evaluation. We were with them daily. One day a fellow student said to me, "See that fellow standing out there under a tree? That's one of my patients. Would you go out there and tell him it's time to come into the ward?" I asked, "Why don't you go after him?" He replied, "I don't have any rapport with him." His reply puzzled me, but I agreed to go. I walked out to where the patient was standing alone in the shade of a tree, and sidled up to him saying, "It's time for you to come into the ward now." Much to my surprise he started toward the door ignoring me. I walked along beside him wondering what to say, relieved at the ease of it all. Suddenly he said, without so much as glancing at me, "Why didn't that other son-of-bitch come after me?" Ever since then I have known what it is *not* to have rapport with a person. You will note he said *that other* not just *that*. There was no mistaking what he thought of both of us.

The interpersonal relationship may be positive or negative. Rapport by definition means only positive feeling. When counseling begins, the feelings may be positive, negative or neutral; that is, neither like nor dislike. Very quickly, the reaction pattern becomes positive or negative. When I was a hospital chaplain, a doctor asked me to see his seriously ill patient. I went to the room where his patient, a thirty-year-old woman with bright and alert eyes and a thin weakened body, lay facing the door. Before I could introduce myself she asked, "Who are you?" I said, "I'm the minister of the hospital." Without a smile, and this was significant, she retorted, "I don't like ministers." (Negative!) I responded, "There are some of them I don't like either. Why don't you like them?" (Acceptance of her statement, identification with her, quickly giving her back the conversation which indicated no desire to dominate and no defensiveness.) Thereafter, the relationship built steadily until within a few weeks it was not uncommon for the nurse to call me and say, "Marion can't get to sleep. Would you come and have a prayer with her?" A quiet greeting, a few words of reassurance and a prayer of quietness in which we reached out in the ancient words familiar to Marion and she would drop off to sleep, content in the assurance of God's enfolding love. She died peaceably some weeks later. And yet, she didn't like ministers. Behind her rebellion was the dislike for her own minister who was dominating and rigid; a man wholly insecure in his relation to people.

Children and youth who have been deeply hurt by people they would normally trust find it difficult to develop a positive interpersonal relationship. Counseling them is a slow process, since they hold everyone at arm's length. They are fearful of being hurt again. These are the shy people, the withdrawn, the caustic, the ill mannered, the aggressive, the bullies. They virtually dare others to like them. Their behavior pattern may be one of open warfare against society or it may show up as withdrawal behind strong defenses. They need help in developing positive interpersonal relationships which they must test over and over again. This throws a considerable weight of responsibility upon the counselor. The average pastor, without extensive specialized training, would do well to avoid working with people with such deeply-rooted emotional disturbances. At the same time, "to whom shall they go?" In many communities there is no available source of professional help. Is the pastor then to reject them? Is he to avoid the risk of a dependency which will develop, if he takes time to work with these persons? In his marriage counseling, the minister will see such people. They are the independent, standoffish, couldn't-care-less kind of persons who dare anyone to love them and who give little affection themselves, except to their children.

In personal crises, the minister faces yet another kind of resistance as he seeks to establish a relationship. A head nurse spoke to me as I was walking down the hospital corridor, "Chaplain, I wish you would see Mr. Blank in Room 226. His wife died shortly after being admitted to the hospital after an accident two nights ago. He blames the doctors for her death." I went to his room. He was a solidly built man in his forties, lying with his head slightly elevated and an unmistakable scowl on his face. I came along side his bed, pulled up a chair and said as I sat down, "Mr. Blank, I'm Mr. Dicks, the minister of the hospital. I heard about your accident and I just came by to sit with you for a little while." Tears came to his eyes as he nodded, saying slowly, "I guess I need a minister. . . . I've been very bitter. . . . I've blamed the doctors, I've blamed myself and I've blamed God."

The story came. He and his wife had been on a holiday in Florida and were returning to their home in New York City. He was driving late at night to make up for lost time. A truck had stopped on the highway and the driver had not had time to put out warning lights before the collision occurred. Mr. Blank's wife was seriously injured and he had been badly bruised with lacerations around the face and arms. They had a child in New York. The child would need its mother.

"If only I had stopped for the night," he said, "if only I had stopped for gas, if, if, if, and then I realize nothing could have prevented it if it was God's will." When I got up to leave he thanked me. I had come simply to *sit* with him, and even if he had said nothing, I would have remained for awhile and then left. In my experience, it has never happened that way. There was always an opening wedge, always the opportunity to help.

NOT BY MORTAL MAN ALONE

In the crisis of life, when sadness has its way with us, when our hearts are heavy and the long thoughts of loneliness claim us, we welcome the trusted friend or the sympathetic stranger who walks, or sits, or waits with us.

We do not want words except as they are our own; we do not want platitudinous phrases that pass our suffering on quickly to God, whom we may hate as of the moment as we hate all goodness, joy and creativity. We are trapped in the dark mood of despair—we feel alone. Our hearts cry out, the hollow empty cry of hurt. If you can quiet your mind and spirit as you come to us, to hold the tender anguished moments of our sorrow, we welcome you. It will not be for long if you enter here. If you come with harshness, with quick movements and hurried, anxious words it is far better that you stay away. If you are of God you will not be afraid. Your spirit will be quiet and your listening heart will take the sadness in a way you know, but may not understand, and rest it in the storeroom of your faith, where it will remain perhaps for all eternity. If you have no such storeroom where you deposit sadness, do not come to me when I am hurt. And do not seek to lift my spirit all too quickly when I mourn the passing of my loved ones, for the grief of separation is not quickly to be shunned away.

When I am dying come to me with joy, not with quick laughter nor with darts of jest; come with joy not to remind me of separation, but of hope fulfilled. When I suffer grief because of loved ones gone in death or distance come with quiet spirit for I am sad; I feel the quick sharp thrusts of hurt; in time my loneliness will mellow. Walk with me but do not hurl your trite words against my weakened soul. Loss through separation for whatever cause is death to me; death to my spirit and my soul; death to companionship and close arms in love.

Do not talk to me of sin when I have sinned; talk to me of hope when I confess. Do not shame my shame filled mind, and thrust me deeper into loneliness; show me the way and give me strength, to stand again and walk with confidence. When I am angry let me vent my hate, to free my burdened feelings from the barbs that penetrate my soul, my heart, my hope and joy. When I am lonely and feel sorry for myself, when the devils of my lesser self arise, do not rebuke but wait patiently, and do not think me only coward; a stronger self will soon arise, the heated moments soon will pass, and pass more quickly then by far, because you wait and trust and listen through the gloom. You hope, you smile, you nod; you suffer, too, with me. Surely then your waiting and your patience is of God; no mortal man can know these things alone, no mortal touch alone can heal.

EIGHT

BUILDING
the INTERPERSONAL RELATIONSHIP

Disciplined Conversation

1. Ask a question
2. Art of Supposing
3. Reflect
4. Grunt
5. Waiting silence
6. Prayer
7. Make another appointment
8. Refer
9. Leave or end interview

Don Beatty is reputed to have said that the mark of a professional person is whether he runs his job or whether the job runs him. The same test applies to the pastoral call and the interview. Are you effective and masterful in your pastoral ministry? Do you proceed in an easy, permissive manner that wins confidence without the loss of direction or leadership? Can you maintain disciplined control of your own feelings so that the counselee can comfortably unburden himself through the course of the interview? The answers you can honestly give to these questions will determine what helps you most need for successful counseling.

Every counseling situation is an interpersonal relationship. It begins with the first spoken word. The counselor's own attitude will largely determine the emotional climate of the first and subsequent sessions. It is important, therefore, that the counselor understand what tools are available to him.

The Question

The question is one of the pastor's most useful tools; it can be harmful as well as helpful. The surgeon knows what to cut and what not to cut. In similar fashion, the skillful pastor is one who knows what to ask and what not to ask. Just as the surgeon has a knowledge of time and the limits of time within which he must work, so the pastor must have a knowledge of when to ask as well as what to ask.

Counseling involves human emotions. (Here I use the word counseling to describe a process in both calling and the more formal conversation which takes place in the pastor's office. The same skills are used and the same problems may be dealt with in the home, the hospital or the office.) In counseling we are more interested in how you feel about an act than in a description of that act; in how you feel about an active relationship than the fact that it is happening; in why you behave in a certain way than the obvious fact that you do. The question is the best technique we have for getting at feelings and in keeping the conversation structured and on a single track. At the same time, we permit but we do not require a person to tell us facts as we focus our attention upon feelings.

An attorney with some training and experience in counseling recently came to our office and told us that ministers could not effectively counsel because they are moralistic. Thus, he would hold that the minister cannot deal with adulterers because he must reject them for such wrongdoing. One might as illogically say that the doctor should not treat disease because doctors first described illness.

A psychiatrist lecturing to my former students illustrated the distinction between his work and ours in this manner. "A woman comes to me and says I have had sexual intercourse with three different men. My response would be, 'What is the problem?' " Then he asked the class of ministers, "What would be your response?" One of the students held up his hand and said, "The same as yours. What else could it be?"

Another psychiatrist becoming familiar with the modern technique of pastoral care asked, "If ministers aren't going to tell people when they are doing wrong, who is?" I am inclined to ask, "What is wrong?" As Pilate asked, "What is truth?"

(1) **The general, non-threatening question.** This is the question used in launching a conversation in a normal situation where one is getting acquainted. Isn't it a pretty day? Who do you think will win the World Series? Do you watch T.V.? How long have you lived here? The general question is not particularly useful but may be important when you are in serious doubt as to a person's response

to you. It is a way of showing interest in a person, an opening of the door. If you receive a negative response or no response at all, you can back off without embarrassment.

(2) **The information question.** This is a question that has many uses: to express your interest, to gain information, to guide the conversation, to slow the conversation up when too much emotion is coming out, to explore feelings without making a direct approach to them. It is asked so that it can be answered on the basis of known information without revealing feeling. What is your work? Do you have a family? How old are your children? Did you sleep well last night? Have you lost weight? Have you been to the fair? How was the traffic last night? Does your husband talk with you? How is companionship in the marriage? Is the sexual side of your marriage satisfying?

The more personal the question the closer you are to the dynamics or the feelings of a person. At any time, the information question may lead into feelings, therefore it is important to move with the response.

(3) **The feeling, or dynamic question.** This question deals with the emotions and it is here that we are most likely to be helpful, since people live by their emotions rather than their intellect. Highly trained engineers, accustomed to deal with facts, think with their emotions when dealing with a wife or a family. The feeling question is used only when the counselor-counselee relationship is well established and both are comfortable in the relationship. At the same time, such questioning strengthens the relationship and carries it further. It enables the counselor to move along and ask: How do you feel about it? What does this mean to you? How did your mother and father get along? How did you feel when your father left? Are you able to give love? What does the church mean to you?

It is interesting to note that discussion of God, Christ and feelings about the church seem to be more personal and more emotionally loaded than a discussion of sexual intercourse.

"We are forthright and honest in sharing our feelings only if we trust the person who presumes to intrude into our secrets, for such intrusion may be very threatening to us, threatening because it forces us to look at ourselves on the one hand and because it trusts our interests to another person. Our trust is influenced by the degree of acceptance we sense in an interrogator, particularly when we are trapped in desperation.

In this connection the student of interpersonal relations would do well to bear in mind that lying is defensive behavior; it is the individual's effort to protect himself, and we should view it as such, not as something evil in itself. Life is an on-going stream and no single event destroys it, not even suicide.

Lying takes many forms. Failure to talk when one needs to talk is lying; boastful talk when one is afraid is lying; blaming a mate for one's own failures in marriage is lying; abusive action toward another person is lying; gossip is lying and that means *all* gossip; distorting the truth to our advantage is lying. We lie because we dare not tell the truth.

To force a person to tell the truth when he is afraid is to do him spiritual harm; to enable him to tell the truth through his trust in you when he is afraid is to help him, *providing* you are courageous enough to accept the dependency he will immediately feel toward you. The *dynamic* question is a sharp and dangerous tool.[1]

(4) **The art of supposing.** Direct questions often will not get at a problem or bring out feelings, particularly when the relationship is infirm or when a person is evasive about his feelings. Then, a different method may be used. One that we have found productive is what may be called the "art of supposing." This method amounts to edging your way into another's anxieties and loneliness. Consider the following suppositions: "I expect you miss your husband when he is away so much." If she does, she will agree; if she doesn't, she will either not respond or give some such answer as, "Not necessarily." One might now simply respond with an "Oh," and wait. The results are often quite meaningful. In either case, you are expressing interest in the parishioner.

"I suppose that a lot of people have asked you about your accident." "I expect you didn't sleep much last night." "I suppose there are times when you feel like telling people what you think of them." "I expect you feel angry at everybody, including God." This method shows understanding; it must be backed up with the ability to wait out a silence while the counselee reflects upon his answer. It is use-

[1] *How to Make Pastoral Calls for Ministers and Laymen,* by Russell L. Dicks (St. Louis, Bethany Press, 1962).

ful with sensitive and fearful persons and is valuable when the counselor can observe and recall a response from one interview to another. In recalling specific responses the written record, which will be discussed later, becomes essential.

(5) **Reflect.** The method of restating the counselee's thought back to him was made popular by Dr. Karl Rogers and his followers. It first came into wide attention through his book *Counseling and Psychotherapy.*[2] Reflection serves to restate the counselee's thought in clear and forthright terms. The counselee recognizes that the counselor understands. Furthermore, this method keeps the pattern of the discussion in focus. One obvious weakness is that the counselor often seems to be behind the counselee and that he does not have an opinion. It is a useful procedure when the conversation moves freely and when emotionally charged material is being discussed. It is not effective in starting a conversation or in expressing concern. Correlated with other methods, it can be most useful, particularly when the counselor is in doubt.

(6) **Grunt.** One of the most useful and descriptive methods in disciplined conversation which always brings a chuckle when described is the response not more nor less than the simple *grunt.* There are different kinds of responsive grunts—"Oh," the surprised response, with raised eyebrows and a rising inflection of the voice; the disappointed "Oh" with dropping voice inflection and sober facial expression; the "Oohh," with sustained voice and a turn of the head, which might be called the searcher's tone; the shamer's "Ohh," with a shaking of the head and a sad face, that is seldom used in counseling, but often in general communication.

There are multiple other variations of the grunt such as the responsive "Uh," which also can run the gamut of acceptance, delight, encouragement, indifference, disappointment, and denial. Other possible responses are: You did? You did. I'll bet you did. You didn't? The response, *of course,* can be used in many ways from derision to joyfulness.

No matter which variant is employed, the grunt is a quick word of response that neither retards nor blocks the conversation. One must be mindful of the revealing nature of intonation. Attitudes are readily communicated by the tone of voice. Such description may

[2] Boston, Houghton Mifflin Company, 1942.

appear to be unimportant. In actual fact, this is an area where most counselors can benefit by self-evaluation and practiced control.

(7) **Waiting silence.** The deliberate use of silence is the counselor's waiting out the counselee's slow thinking-process when he gropes for the right word, thought or feeling. Such gaps in the counseling session may occasionally be closed by the use of questions and reflections. Several years ago a major school of social work emphasized the use of waiting silence as an all-out method. The experiment was short-lived and ended in failure. It did, however, help the social worker of that era to correct a practice that was too aggressive and directive. Soon afterward, the emphasis was put upon insight and the study of psychiatry. A parallel trend developed in the clinical pastoral education movement.

I have found the judicious use of silence to be most productive. Considerable discipline on the part of the counselor is necessary, before this practice can be rewarding. Whenever the counselee is thinking and searching for a word or idea, the counselor waits. When, however, the counselee is not thinking or deliberately withholds communication, such moments of silence are non-productive. Like the little grunts of encouragement previously described, silence is given content by the counselor's nods of approval and by his eyes. Here one must guard against staring. The fixed stare is annoying and disruptive to the counselee. It is better to look at him then slowly look away. Return your glance in a natural manner. You nod, approve, encourage, and think *with* him. Avoid thinking *for* him when the decision should be that of the counselee. Counseling deals with his problem which is yours to share only in a privileged manner. The artful counselor avoids taking over the problem to the extent that the counselee stops working upon it himself and sits back to let you do the job.

(8) **Prayer.** Prayer is mentioned here simply to position it in its proper relationship to other techniques in the interpersonal relationship. It will be discussed fully in the next chapter.

(9) **Make another appointment.** When in doubt, make another appointment. Few pastoral situations can adequately be handled in one session. A follow-up appointment is easily indicated by the parting words, "I will see you again soon." If the call is upon a sick or convalescing person, care should be taken to avoid setting a specific time for revisiting unless you are quite certain you will be

able to fulfill the appointment. With a seriously ill person you may say, "I will see you this evening," or "the first thing in the morning." You must then be certain to do so. The sick person will remember the promise and look forward to your next call. A broken promise is virtually inexcusable in the mind of the seriously ill person.

In formal counseling, follow-up appointments are important. The continuing relationship which indicates the counselor's concern is reassuring. Timing the appointments is a part of managing the relationship. I often point out to a counselee that some of the most important gains in counseling often take place between interviews. During this interval, the counselee continues to rethink and restructure his problem. The counselor may wisely and helpfully say, "I need to think about this for awhile."

Ordinarily, appointments are spaced one week apart. Exceptions concern serious emotional upsets, mild depression and marital discord that threatens to break a marriage. In such instances, appointments are stepped up during the acute phase of the situation. Properly spaced appointments serve to prevent unhealthy dependency relationships. While the counselor may say, "Call me if you need to," he should recognize that excessive telephone calls between appointments are not emergency calls. However, it is expedient that the counselor be available for calls from the person who has a tendency to be depressed or who is temporarily isolated in a destructive marriage relationship.

I heard recently of a psychiatrist who never discharged anyone from psychotherapy. The only way they could terminate the sessions was to stop of their own accord. The tendency to cling to counselees is a mark of immaturity on the part of the counselor. When I first began counseling in private practice where a fee is charged, my tendency was to discharge people too soon. Experience is the great teacher here. Many people will follow your guidance saying, "I will come as long as you think it necessary." Not infrequently, I will say when the counseling is nearing completion (this is never done in the early part of the counseling), "Do you think you need another appointment next week?" Here, the fee is a valuable aid in controlling the relationship.

(10) **Refer.** The pastor ought to be aware of available resources for referral—doctors, psychiatrists, social agencies, counseling centers,

attorneys, A.A.'s, homes for unmarried mothers, hospitals. Wisdom and strategy in referral is good counseling procedure just as it is good medical practice. The doctor who never refers is not much of a doctor, just as the pastor who never refers is not much of a counselor. A doctor friend of mine in Chicago said, "If I make a referral and the patient recovers, I get the credit because I had the good judgment to refer to a competent person. If the patient dies, I am not blamed because I recognized the seriousness of the case."

Referral is never interpreted as lack of competence on your part. "I want you to talk to a doctor I know who specializes in this kind of problem." If it is a psychiatrist, you may have to be more tactful, for the public image and stereotype of the psychiatrist is not always informed or flattering. In marital quarreling when one mate wants to say something really devastating he or she says, "You need to see a psychiatrist. You're crazy." Psychiatrists deal with people who are emotionally upset as well as those who are mentally sick.

The depressed person usually accepts referral readily, for he needs and desires help. The schizophrenic rejects referral, since he often fails to recognize his illness for what it is. The schizophrenic with depression will frequently seek help. If his hallucinations have a religious orientation, the counselee will often resist psychiatric referral. The pastor must use whatever skills he can to induce such a person to accept outside help. Since schizophrenics often have poor interpersonal relationships, the counseling situation is greatly strained. When in doubt refer, and when not in doubt refer.

The pastor would do well to refer most of his marital situations for counseling although my observation is that it is this group that the pastor is least likely to refer. Everybody presumes to be an expert on marriage; so more and more marriages die each year.

Marriage counseling is an extremely difficult art and the local pastor has neither the time nor the skill to do much with people in serious marital difficulties. Furthermore, the distressed couple often have problems of an intimate and personal nature which they prefer not to discuss with the pastor whom they see weekly and under whose direction they worship.

As marriage counseling develops and as counseling centers are established, the pastor will have more outside assistance with these problems. At present he may have to do the best he can.

(11) **Leave, or end the interview.** The pastor often finds it difficult to end a call in the sick room or home, just as he finds it difficult to end an office interview. The termination of a call or interview is as important as its beginning. It seems simple enough to be able to say, "I must go now. I will see you again soon," and stand up and leave. In actual practice, it is not. Referring to their formal counseling I find pastors asking, "How do you get them to stop talking?" or saying, "I talked to her for three hours." Here is evidence of weak leadership and mismanagement.

Keep the purpose of your call clearly in mind. The house call is intended to establish a contact and build the relationship. Sickroom calls serve to support and encourage. Whenever counseling would appear to be helpful, as it often is, the caller must be conscious of the patient's strength. It is wise to consult the patient's doctor before permitting him to engage in even a thirty-minute conversation. As the conversation lags due to the patient's fatigue, it is time to leave whether he has stopped talking or not. Then, you take control. Stand, if you have been sitting, and say, "I must go now, we will talk again soon." If you have read the signs indicating that prayer is desired, pray. Be alert for any quick confession which may come after the prayers. Then, go to the door and leave. It is that simple; but, it must be done with confidence. At no time should the impression be given of rejection or uncertainty, or busyness.

In office counseling when you have no secretary to "buzz you" you will say, "We have talked an hour which is as long as we should at one time. (You do not say why.) I would like to see you again next Tuesday," and you make your appointment. Sometimes the conversation has not reached a natural termination point at the end of an hour. You indicate, by looking at your watch, that time is running out. You may say, "We must stop soon now." Soon you stand up. Or, you may say, "We will talk more about this next time," indicating that the subject is not closed.

It is important to control your work schedule for the sake of the counselee, as well as yourself. Some people are completely disorganized and undisciplined in the scheduling of their time. By working in an orderly way, the counselor gets the point across that life, work, hate, love and conversation exist within the boundaries of time. If you, yourself, have no sense of time, do not become a pastor counselor.

The interpersonal relationship is so important in counseling it may be identified as the Grace of God leavening this ministry of healing. The counselor must seek to study and understand this force. Despite persistent efforts at self-improvement in the art of counseling, many counselors experience difficulties in certain relationships. The problem area may relate to counseling the person of position, the skeptic, the flirtatious woman, the alcoholic and so on. In any such relationship, the counselor will seek to understand his own feelings and develop his art of communication. The counselor's self-understanding and skills are channels of healing.

NINE

PRAYER

Prayer is the minister's unique method in helping people. He, alone, of the helping persons will use this method in his ministrations. It is highly important that he thoroughly understand the use and value of prayer in counseling. Through prayer, the pastor directs a relationship between the individual and God. In so doing, the pastor steps out of his active role as counselor into the interpersonal relationship. Although the pastor is physically present, the setting takes on a new dimension whereby the person in need now experiences an awareness of a relationship toward God. The pastor then becomes an onlooker, an activator, a medium for the Grace of God. He can still short-circuit the flow of God into a person, but he is not responsible for the fact of God and the healing redemptive power of God as it enfolds a suffering person. The pastor merely throws the switch that releases the God strength much as does the engineer who presses the button that releases the flow of electricity.

While the engineer does not create electricity, he does select the circuits that direct its flow. So also must the pastor understand and meet certain conditions in his use of prayer in pastoral care. Four basic considerations can provide helpful insights. It will be helpful to consider:

1. What prayer is;
2. When to use prayer in pastoral work;
3. The conditions of prayer;
4. The contents of prayer.

1. **What prayer is.** Prayer is manifest in many forms. The violinist drawing from his instrument the clear tones that carry the message of the composer is communicating with God; the baby crying in the night, the weeping mother in her loneliness; the clasp of

two lovers in the ecstasy of affection—all may be prayer. The form of prayer as we conceive of it in pastoral care, is the uniting of the pastor's concern with the evident needs of the suffering person. This is the pastor's silent or voiced prayer—directed Godward. In other words, one prays the prayer that the parishioner himself might pray, if he were articulate and free from stress of the moment. Panic, fever, drugs, dullness, anger, anxiety and discouragement appear in one form or another to blunt one's feelings toward God so that he cannot pray. We can understand why, on occasion, the sense of God's presence slips away. Further, a pastor's prayer, when one feels isolated from the customary place of prayer and the people with whom one customarily prays, renews one's spiritual sensitivity. The crises of illness, death and grief intrude to the degree where one's God consciousness becomes remote. The pastor's prayer reduces the tensions of the moment and restores perspective.

2. **When to use prayer in pastoral work.** The most frequent occasions when the pastor will pray orally in pastoral calling and counseling will be: in routine calling; when calling upon the sick; in ministering to the dying; with the bereaved; and calling upon older people. Only occasionally will he offer a prayer in formal counseling. Such occasions will relate to moments during premarital instruction, the discussing of church membership with a person or couple, and the time of departure to or return from military service. The opportunity is present whether the conference be in the home or the church office. The listed categories apply primarily to the pastor's work with his own parishioners. Through the custom of offering a brief prayer during routine calls where no stress is present, the minister establishes the practice of prayer and himself as a person of prayer. Thereafter, it will be natural for his parishioners to accept and expect pastoral prayers during their moments of crisis.

The pastor should always be alert not to embarrass his sick parishioner in a hospital ward by suggesting prayer at an inopportune moment when undue attention would be attracted. This applies especially in the case of the shy person. Whenever there is considerable noise and distraction as would be true during regular visiting hours, it will be hard to achieve the degree of quietness necessary for effective prayer. Whenever distractions of this nature exist, it is easy to say to a person, "I will remember you in my prayers later."

I have often advocated that the pastor have a supply of prayer cards with him as he makes his visits. Such a card might then be given to the patient. The prayer card should be neatly printed and of a convenient size, so that it can be placed beside a water glass or used as a bookmark, and where it can be easily seen or glanced at in quiet moments. The printed prayer need not be of your own composition, but it should carry your name, such as, "Presented by . . ."

The minister will have occasion to call upon many who are non-parishioners not only in his evangelistic calling, but in the sick room and upon grief suffering persons who have come to his attention usually through suggestions from his church members. Many ministers are undecided as to the propriety of offering to pray with these persons. If one bears in mind the following conditions, he will be right ninety to ninety-five per cent of the time.

Any procedures that can simplify your decisions will be welcome assets, for decision making takes its toll in time and energy. This is true in general. All of us follow much the same rituals in dressing. Well established habits relieve us of having to rethink every course of action. If you had daily to decide the specific mode and manner for washing, dressing and grooming, a great deal of valuable time and energy would be wasted. The same is true in trying to decide—Shall I pray, or not? Will the patient welcome prayer? Will it be embarrassing? Will it upset him? I have had, as many experienced ministers can independently affirm, instances where my prayer has done harm. Almost all of my ministry has been served in working with other people's parishioners where the risks of the wrong decision are greater than with one's own people who know and love you; provided you have served them well. If not, they can be critical, disinterested and unresponsive.

Signs That Indicate Prayer with Non-parishioners

(1) If a person welcomes you with some show of enthusiasm as you introduce yourself as a minister, such as saying, "It's nice of you to come to see me. I'm glad to meet you" and smiles and greets you cordially, you will know immediately he is being more than just polite. There may even be some show of emotion such as tears. Remember what was said earlier about pre-counseling influence.

(2) If he uses the language of religion or makes reference to his

own spiritual needs or religious affiliations, such as, "I wondered if ministers ever come here to call." "I guess I need to talk with a minister." "I've been lying here praying that someone like you would come by." "I haven't been going much to church in recent years and I'm sorry I haven't."

(3) If he tells you anything that is personal, revealing concern or anxiety about himself or his family, such as, "I wish the operation could be put off until my son returns from the army." "I have delayed coming to the hospital as long as I could because I was afraid of what they would find." "My daughter is not getting along well with her husband."

(4) And, of course, if a person sends for a minister before an operation or during a long convalescence, he will want you to have prayer with him. He may want to make confession. All people make confessions of one sort or another, and they prefer to make them to one who is professionally qualified to listen, understand and respond in a helping way. If he makes a confession, he will want a prayer at its end. The prayer has the effect of absolution when it embodies the elements of God's understanding and forgiveness. Prayers of absolution are especially important for those seriously ill persons who seek to clear their consciences when death is imminent.

You will quickly learn to detect these signs which will become a natural part of your approach to the pastoral task. Probably one out of three or four of your contacts in the pastoral ministry will be made with non-members of the church you serve.

3. **The conditions of prayer.** The first condition of effective pastoral prayer is quietness; quietness of spirit on the part of the pastor. This is communicated by modulation of voice and the careful choice of words. The possible distractions in the hospital ward are physical conditions that cannot usually be controlled. I sometimes think the signs one sees "Quiet, sickness" should be hung inside hospitals.

This needed quietness is achieved most easily by the minister after he has suggested prayer by his consciously relaxing his own tension. There follows the relaxation of bodily tension within a matter of seconds. The minister's own sense of relaxation and self-forgetfulness are reflected in the serenity of his bearing and his voice.

Henry Sloan Coffin was fond of saying that the language of public prayer is that of lyric poetry. Any word out of place in a lyric poem would be out of place in a public prayer. Few clergy write and publish poetry, but this does not outrule the capacity to be poetic. Most pastors can and do cultivate a sensitivity to the language of prayer.

A scriptural phrase or verse woven into one's direct address to the Divine, or the early sentences of a prayer will help achieve the phraseology of poetic prayer.

4. **The contents of prayer.** The pastoral prayer must recognize realities of the situation and the needs of the parishioner. While pain and guilt feelings may be present, the prayer must not only lift these up to God but move ahead in positive terms of acceptance and the joyfulness of faith. Death is not tragic, if it draws one closer to God. The pastor, himself, must believe this and instill this attitude within the mind of his parishioner so that he looks toward the life to come in confidence.

Suitable prayers for specific situations, and appropriate scriptural readings are provided in the following section. They have been effectively used in my own ministry and will help to illustrate the application of the principles set forth in this chapter.

FOR ONE WHO KNOWS HE IS DYING

The Lord is my light and my salvation; whom shall I fear?
The Lord is the strength of my life; of whom shall I be afraid?
Though an host encamp against me, my heart shall not fear; though war should rise against me, even then will I be confident.
For in the time of trouble he shall hide me in his pavilion; in the secret of his tabernacle shall he hide me; he shall set me up upon a rock.
Teach me Thy way, O Lord, and lead me in a plain path.
I had fainted, unless I had believed to see the goodness of the Lord, in the land of the living.
Wait on the Lord: be of good courage, and he shall strengthen thine heart: wait, I say, on the Lord.

Psalm 27 Selected

Almighty God, Eternal Companion, Creator and Preserver of life,[1]
Giver of friendship, Author of all affection:
Thou who dost support us with the strength of the Everlasting Arms,
We rest in Thee and Thou dost bear us up,
We rest in Thee and Thou dost renew us,
As the earth is reborn in the spring,
With the coming of new life;
As the bird flies and comes to rest in its nest,
So we are renewed in our faith,
So we rest in Thy affection.

Bless this dear one, our Father,
Take from him all regret,
Hear his confession of whatever failures have been his
And claim him for Thyself.
Accept him as he returns home,
Even as the father welcomes the returning son,
As the daughter returns to the arms of a loving mother.

Bless his loved ones and keep them,
As he has kept them in his affection.
May they know that he had but gone on before them,
That he will prepare a place for them
Even as our Lord, Jesus Christ, has prepared
A place for all who follow in faith.

Now give us hope and peace and confidence,
That will sustain us in the Life Everlasting,
Through Jesus Christ, our Lord.
The Lord bless you and keep you;
The Lord make His face to shine upon you and be gracious unto you;
The Lord lift up His countenance upon you and give you peace;
Both now and forevermore. Amen.

[1] *Comfort Ye My People*, Russell L. Dicks (New York, The Macmillan Company, 1947).

A PRAYER FOR ONE DYING

Eternal God, Father of us all,
Thou who dost lead us beside the still waters of the spirit,
And dost make us to lie down in green pastures of the soul,
We turn to Thee in quietness and confidence,
Thanking Thee for the gift of life and the strength of faith.
We confess our sins, acknowledging that we have done things we ought not to have done,
And have been willful to follow our desires rather than Thy will,
Have mercy upon us and grant us Thy forgiveness.
We pray for the joys of heaven for ourselves and our loved ones.
Keep them in Thy sure affection,
And unite us with them in faith.
Through Jesus Christ, we pray.
Amen.

A PRAYER FOR ONE WHO IS SICK

Almighty God, Father, Creator, Sustainer of life,
Thou who has breathed into us the strength of life
And has given us the gift of health,
We quiet our spirits, we give over the heated moments and rest in Thee.
Thou who dost seek to make us well and whole,
We thank Thee for all who serve Thee through the healing forces—doctors, nurses and all who serve here.
Support their wisdom, patience and skill;
We remember our loved ones,
Keep them in Thy affection,
And grant us a confidence and a freedom from anxiety,
That Thy healing spirit may fill our spirits
And make us whole again,
Through Jesus Christ our Lord.
Amen.

THE HEART CRIES OUT TO GOD

Prayer has been called the soul's sincere desire. While we believe God does not determine the time and place of our death and the death of our loved ones, He does hold us in His love as He does here. Therefore, it is reasonable and desirable to pray for the dead. There are few such prayers in Protestant devotional literature, aside from the funeral prayer, and it is largely centered in the prayer for the grief-suffering person, with some expression of gratitude for the life and heroism of the departed.

It is not with any thought of changing the will of God that we pray for our loved ones who have died; it is to give thought and expression to the grief-suffering person's yearning—the speaking of heart to heart.

We think in human terms when we think of immortality. What other terms do we have? Are the things of the spirit so different from the things of the flesh? Our prayers are cast in human terms and we trust God to understand and accept the longings of our hearts.

It is important to remember that the ones we love are not buried in the ground. . . . In the course of more than twenty-five years as a hospital chaplain I have stood beside many at the time of their death. There one is able to observe that the difference between life and death is of the spirit, in the capacity to feel and to express feelings—the giving and receiving of love. This capacity does not die—this feeling is not buried; it lives on in God.

So we pray to God in behalf of those who are with Him and in behalf of ourselves.

PRAYER WITH THE PARENTS OF A BABY

Oh Thou from whom cometh every good and perfect gift:
The light of the morning, the cool of the evening, the warmth of the
    noonday sun,
The laughter of a child, and the smile of a baby,
Hold this baby, Oh God, in Thy gracious love;

Please God, if she should cry at night
May she be held by some kind mother there
Who will love her as she has been loved;
Knowing this we will rest better when we think of her.
She is so dainty, so helpless, and so very small,
Be sure that she is warm at night;
And please, dear God, if you would be so kind,
Could she have a light on in the hall?
Amen.

PRAYER WITH THE PARENTS OF A LITTLE GIRL

Eternal God and Father of us all,
Thou in whom we rest and from whom we draw our courage, strength and hope,
We trust a little girl in Thee for only Thou canst know her need,
Her happy smile, her zest, her joy;
In Thy care and tender love keep her through the night and through the day;
She loved a cat, a dog, a pony, and a doll,
And many friends—she loved to play at many things.
In Thy heavenly home give her a home,
In Thy heavenly ways make strong her ways,
Enfold her in Thy affection,
And wrap her in a father's and mother's sure support;
For she was more than life to us,
Keep her, Father, in Thy love.
Amen.

PRAYER WITH THE PARENTS OF A BOY

O Thou Spirit beyond our spirit and Hope beyond our hope,
Accept a boy into Thy heavenly affection,
And encircle him with Thy gracious love;

Fill his day with happy things a boy would like to do—
Give him trees to climb, and pools in which to swim,
And baseballs to chase in the afternoon.
In the evening as his steps carry him to Thee
Caress him with a mother's tender touch,
And care for him with a father's tender care;
Give him companionship, O God,
And in the night grant him the certainty of a warm and friendly home.
If he should cry at night, or hurt,
Be Thou his nurse and mother, Lord,
And may he know we hold him in our hearts.
Amen.

PRAYER FOLLOWING THE DEATH OF A MOTHER

Thou who art rest at the end of the day
And the strength of the early morning,
Thou who are ease from the hurt
And comfort for the sorrowing,
Bestow upon this mother Thy most gracious welcome.
She will be at home in heaven, Eternal God,
For hers has been the thought and effort of an angel creature,
As she has comforted us, so, please God, comfort her;
As she has encouraged us, bound up our hurts,
And sent us on our way, so, God, may she be encouraged.
Give her ease from the day's long doings,
And when she is rested may she pass through the heavenly vistas
To friends and loved ones,
And share with them in a time of eternal rejoicing.
Give us the will to share her tenderness,
And grant us the patience to know her patience,
That we, like she, may seek to live a courageous life,
Until the evening comes and the shadows fall.
Amen.

A FRIEND'S PRAYER FOR A FRIEND

Eternal and Everlasting God,
Thou who knowest the depth of our feelings
And the breadth of our sadness
When friend leaves friend;
As the shadows fall and night moves across the sky,
As the evening lights fail and darkness closes around us,
We wait with quiet longing as emptiness encircles us.
We have walked many paths together,
Sat in cool evenings and shared long thoughts with each other,
As heart speaks to heart, so friend knows friend;
Now at the time of separation we commend his spirit to Thy spirit;
Eternal God, claim him for Thyself,
And may his joy be joyfulness complete in Thee;
May his mind search through the highways of Thy thoughts,
And may his spirit find companionship with Thee,
O God, Companion of our years, and Friend to all who seek Thee.
Amen.

A PASTOR'S PRAYER FOR A PARISHIONER

Eternal God, Lord and Father of mankind,
Thou who dost support us at all times,
And who dost comfort us when grief overtakes us,
We thank Thee for the gift of life and the strength of faith,
Faith that bears us up when our hearts are sad,
Faith that sustains us when we are tired;
We rejoice in the hope of Christian immortality,
And we rejoice in the lives of the faithful.
For the life of this one recently gone to Thee we give Thee thanks,
And we pray for his loved ones who walk through the loneliness of separation;
Comfort them, we pray Thee, and make strong their hope,
Accept their grief and give them rest in the night,

May the new day bring a renewal of spirit and a warmth of their love,
Through Jesus Christ, our Lord.
Amen.

FAITH

By faith Abraham, when he was called to go out into a place which he should after receive for an inheritance, obeyed; and he went out, not knowing whither he went.
For he looked for a city which hath foundations, whose builder and maker is God.

Hebrews 11:8, 10

By faith Moses, when he was come to years, refused to be called the son of Pharaoh's daughter;
By faith he forsook Egypt, not fearing the wrath of the king: for he endured, as seeing him who is invisible.

Hebrews 11:24, 27

And what shall I more say? for the time would fail me to tell of Gideon, and of Barak, and of Samson, and of Jephthae; of David also, and Samuel, and of the prophets:
God having provided some better thing for us, that they without us should not be made perfect.

Hebrews 11:32, 40

A PRAYER OF FAITH[2]

Almighty God, Who setteth the planets in their courses and the suns in the heavens, make us to know that we are Thy children. Thou hast called us forth as a part of Thy Creation. Thou Who madest the petals of a flower, the colors of the sunset, the smile of a child, we rest in Thee and Thou dost support us.

Make us to trust Thee as a child trusts its parent. Give us faith to go forth even as Abraham went forth, as Thy people have gone forth with courage in every generation. As we have dwelt in peace

[2] Dicks, *op. cit.*, page 58.

and confidence so may we move forward with hope and joy. Remove from us all regret, cleanse us of every stain, that our minds may be filled with Thy Peace and our spirit filled with Thy Grace.

We commend our loved ones to Thy continued care. We rejoice in the love we have known with them and we pray Thou wilt be their Constant Companion. And make them strong to do Thy Will, through Jesus Christ, our Lord. Amen.

PRAYER WITH AN AGED PERSON[3]

Eternal God, Creator of life, Author of hope,
Giver of spiritual peace and the life everlasting;
Thou has blessed us and renewed our confidence;
Through the years Thou has strengthened us for the day's task,
Comfort this dear one in the days of later maturity.
May the lessons of life bear him up
And may the fullness of faith strengthen him.
With the passing years he has gained wisdom,
Now may communion with Thee guide him in the evening hour.
Reward him through Divine affection
And make him to know a deeper love in Thee.
And give him a vision of the eternity before him;
Support him with the affection of the church invisible
And give him high hope through Jesus Christ, our Lord.
Amen.

THE RIGHTEOUS MAN

Blessed is the man that walketh not in the counsel of the ungodly, nor standeth in the way of sinners, nor sitteth in the seat of the scornful.

But his delight is in the law of the Lord; and in His law doth he meditate day and night.

And he shall be like a tree planted by the rivers of water, that bringeth forth his fruit in his season, his leaf also shall not wither; and whatsoever he doeth shall prosper.

[3] Dicks, *op. cit.*, page 95.

The ungodly are not so: but are like the chaff which the wind driveth away.
Therefore the ungodly shall not stand in the judgment, nor sinners in the congregation of the righteous.
For the Lord knoweth the way of the righteous: but the way of the ungodly shall perish.

Psalm 1

THANKSGIVING FOR AN AGED SAINT[4]

We thank Thee, O God, for this Thy servant; patient in tribulation, rejoicing in hope; continuing instant in prayer; not slothful in business; given to hospitality. Having fought the good fight, and kept the faith grant to him the crown of life that fadeth not away.

Put far from us, O God, all worry and misgiving; that having done our best while it was day, we may, when the night cometh, commit ourselves, our tasks, and those we love, into Thy holy keeping and accept of Thee the gift of sleep. Through Jesus Christ our Lord. Amen.

As many as are led by the Spirit of God, these are sons of God. For ye received not the spirit of bondage again unto fear; but ye received the spirit of adoption, whereby we cry, Abba, Father. The Spirit himself beareth witness with our spirit, that we are children of God: and if children, then heirs; heirs of God, and joint-heirs with Christ; if so be that we suffer with Him, that we may be also glorified with Him. And we know that to them that love God all things work together for good.

Rom. 8:14, 17, 28

BENEDICTION FOR THE AGED

Now unto Him that is able to keep you from falling, and to present you faultless before the presence of His glory with exceeding joy, to the only wise God our Saviour be glory and majesty, dominion and power, both now and ever. Amen.

Jude 1:24, 25

[4] Dicks, *op. cit.*, page 97.

PRAYER OF JOHN HENRY NEWMAN

Lord, support me all day long of this troublous life, until the shadows lengthen and the evening comes, and the busy world is hushed, and the fever of life is over, and my work is done. Then in Thy Mercy grant me a safe lodging, and a holy rest, and peace at the last. Amen, Lord Jesus, Amen.

TEN

RECORDS

The written record is an absolutely essential tool for the minister in his pastoral calling and counseling. It often accounts for the difference between shoddy, careless work and professional disciplined work. Our great advance in pastoral care has come simultaneously with our careful recording and use of written records. The minister has not previously had a place at the conference table where social scientists gathered to discuss modern man and his problems. Whenever fellowships and scholarships were awarded for advanced study and research in the humanities, few were awarded to the clergy. This pattern is gradually changing for the better, and greater recognition of the clergy can be expected in the future. It was recognized that the minister helped people, but neither the minister nor the scholar studying his work had records available for study and evaluation.

In their book, *Casebook in Pastoral Counseling,*[1] Newman S. Cryer, Jr. and John Monroe Vayhinger refer to the launching of the department of pastoral care which I edited and columnized for five years in the monthly magazine, *The Pastor*. The authors reported, "Near the end of World War II an editor and a hospital chaplain began a correspondence that led to the publication of pastoral counseling interviews in *The Pastor,* a magazine for Protestant ministers. For the first time, reports of actual clinical material were made available generally to ministers on a regular basis; and for the first time pastors had a place to which they could send their counseling reports for critical appraisal. Other periodicals since then have inaugurated types of counseling clinics for teaching purposes, but the recorded accounts published in *The Pastor* in 1945 were the earliest to appear regularly in a Protestant journal.

[1] New York (Abingdon Press, 1962) page 5. Used by permission.

"This innovation came at a critical time in the life of the modern clinical pastoral movement. World War II had ended. Chaplains were returning home with a new respect for the skills of counseling. Those who ministered at home became aware of research in psychology and psychiatry and the new approaches to treatment of personality problems. Wartime experiences had led ministers at home and overseas to an appreciation of the fact that people could get help from counseling. Postwar tensions contributed to the rise in the incidence of emotionally disturbed persons and brought to pastors a new understanding of their role in helping them. Pastors were recovering their traditional role in the cure of souls."

Three basic types of records have proved to be helpful to the busy minister in his pastoral work.

Types of Record

1. Notation;
2. Summary;
3. Verbatim.

(1) **The notation record** is the simplest type of record the minister can keep and it is usually kept on a card, 3 x 5 or 5 x 7. The smaller card is more easily handled, but the larger card has the advantage of greater working space. The name, address, telephone number and names of members of the family are listed. Calls are noted by date. Some ministers find it useful to note the type of call and significant data which is often listed by code such as, "Sick Call, a. (anxiety); Routine Call–m.c. (Marital Counseling); Routine Call, worried about daughter, Jane; Routine Call, not at home, left card."

Such a record will accurately reflect calls, visits and interviews. Thus, a check list is available as a guard against oversights in visiting. During my hospital chaplaincy days there were always some on my calling list who I would prefer not to have called on again. Without the check list at hand it would be easy to forget them although I might pass their doors every day. The busy pastor can easily forget certain parishioners, especially the inactive ones and those who show irritation, resistance or criticism to the minister and his program. The notation record is simply your own work tool.

(2) **The summary record** is more elaborate, and is the work-horse type of record for both calling and formal counseling. In counseling it is more elaborate than in calling, for here the pastor may write while the counselee talks. One advantage of recording the interview is that it occupies your eyes while the parishioner is thinking. Beyond that, the counselee senses that you are attentive and concerned with his problem. You will need to make some introductory statement when you begin writing, such as, "I'll jot down some of these things so I will remember them. This is just for my own use and no one else will see them." Be careful not to write down highly personal references having to do with sexual matters, for instance, although this information may be important. If necessary, the information may be added later, and in code. These records should not be given to your secretary to type. Church people are very sensitive about the church secretary and her possible access to confidential material.

The summary record includes whatever you think will be useful for you to remember next week, next month, or even next year. You cannot be sure just when you will need the record, so you will write full notes rather than rely upon memory. Content wise, it will contain both factual material, such as, how long married, names and ages of children, where husband or wife work—and feeling material, such as, how the counselee feels about wife or husband's activities, interests, relatives, drinking, work, attitudes, affections, and, above all, communication between the two. The next person you may visit could have a completely different type of problem. You may now be counseling a young woman with a dating problem. Several appointments later you will be talking about other matters completely unrelated to what has gone before. If you see several people, as you inevitably will, before you see the girl with the dating problem again, you will not remember the specifics of that interview. She will. If you do not remember, you will appear stupid or disinterested. A written summary record will avoid this trap.

The counselor should write summary notes upon his summary record, if only to clarify his own thinking. This device will aid the counselor to better sense and understand the person's needs. Summary notes will prove to be helpful starters for the next session. Such notations need not be any more elaborate than the following suggestions.

> J. is afraid of men, just why I am not sure. Her freezing when a boy puts his arm around her would indicate a deep anxiety. We need to discuss her early feelings toward her father. She needs to develop more self-confidence. Discuss this with her and help her to plan for active participation in young peoples' activities.

The summary record is more useful in formal counseling than in calling because it can be written during the conversation. In the routine calls, one must record notes after he returns to the office. You may have every good resolve to record the data when you get to your car or office, but you will not. We advise the notation record for calling and the summary record for counseling.

(3) **The verbatim record,** which we adopted largely from psychiatric social work was our study teaching research record. Anton Boisen once criticized me in an early clinical pastoral conference by saying, "Dicks, students do not keep records. They simply write down the conversations they have with patients." His students were pouring over the psychiatric, psychological and social histories of patients which were open to them and preparing reproductions of those records, a practice that was as utterly impractical for our work in the general hospital as it is for the work of the minister serving a local church. In time, the chaplain supervisors in the mental hospitals came to insist that their students write verbatim records of their conversations with patients, also. Here, the actual confrontation, the involvement, was reported on paper, thus objectifying the experience which could then be studied and evaluated.

The verbatim record is written after the conversation. It is admitted that the writer does not remember every word and statement made. Nevertheless, he remembers most of the important feelings. Some highly imaginative students may record statements that were not actually made, but should have been. Padding the record is misleading and detrimental to the development of counseling skills.

We advocate the use of the verbatim record for study, procedural evaluation and self-improvement. The pastor with years of experience will use it seldom, but it is very important for the minister in those early years when he seeks to strengthen his role in interpersonal relationships. Most students for the ministry dislike record keeping as do those engaged in the study of social work and medicine. Nevertheless, doctors realize that patient charts and complete medical histories are essential to good medical practice. Good records are equally important to the minister. Do not begrudge the time required to keep them. A fifteen-minute conversation with a person may require as much as an hour for transcription. Those fifteen minutes may be useless in your study of and service to the counselee or patient without proper attention to the hour of record keeping, evaluation and learning.

Such records should always contain a summary in which you ask yourself certain questions which you answer in your summary. (a) We talked about (1), (2), (3); (b) This means (1), (2), (3); (c) We need to explore (1), (2), (3). Not always will a conversation reveal three clearly defined points. On occasion there may be only one central consideration. In some few instances you will be unable to isolate any single pervading thought or pattern. Yet, the data recorded will preserve the essential factors; the certainties, the probabilities and the unknowns.

Bonus benefits come to the pastoral counselor who keeps accurate and complete records. These are psychological and professional in nature. The pastor soon discovers that he is developing a more systematic and orderly approach to his total ministry. Valuable time is saved by improved scheduling for visitation and counseling. There is less evidence of stress and strain in the interpersonal relationships, and in the pastor's own life. Gradually, he learns to make the system serve him. There follows a new sense of self-assurance, poise and mastery. His associates quickly sense his growth and maturity in professional competence.

The magnetic tape is used by some counselors in recording interviews. Aside from the use of recording interviews for research and study purposes this is an unwieldy method necessitating a typing of the material which breaks the confidential nature of the counseling. Also, such a record contains all the chit-chat and small talk in every conversation which is desirable for understanding of the building of a relationship but not necessary for the counselor's own use of the record. Finally, a recording machine often blocks the free flow of confessional material particularly that pertaining to sexual experience and sexual feelings.

A good positive use of the recording machine is in work with alcoholics in which the counselor explains as he turns on the machine, placing it in full view, "I'm going to put our conversation on a record and you and I will listen to it in a few weeks to see what progress we have made." Then in a few weeks the record is listened to by counselee and counselor, often with good results.

ELEVEN

The PERSON *under* PSYCHIATRIC TREATMENT[1]

The pastor is often faced with the question of his relationship to a person undergoing psychiatric treatment. A problem of professional relationship arises when the patient comes to the minister seeking his advice concerning such psychiatric care. More often than not, members of the patient's family will come to the pastor for help.

Psychiatric treatment is still in its infancy, and therapies vary to such a degree that the public is uncertain about them. The pastor is trusted, and in many such instances his advice will be taken seriously, as will that of the family physician. The pastor should no longer shirk such responsibility by pointing out the obvious, "I'm not a psychiatrist, therefore, I don't know." Although he is not a surgeon, the pastor will often recognize a person's need for surgery. He need not be an anatomist or surgeon before encouraging a person to seek and trust good surgical care.

In the following situations, patients under psychiatric treatment will also need pastoral care. This applies whether the patient is hospitalized, under the private care of the practicing psychiatrist or simply in need of such care.

1. The depressed hospitalized patient who is an active church member.
2. The grief suffering person who is not psychotic.
3. The person with marital difficulty who recognizes a need for pastoral help.

1 While we will have one or more books upon the subject of Pastoral Care of the mentally sick, we include a special chapter here by way of a general introduction to this important subject.

4. The person who has broken the law and feels guilty for his act.
5. The person under treatment concerned about his religious faith, who attributes his condition to unbelief.
6. The person who has guilt feelings about an attempt at suicide.
7. The emotionally unstable person with guilt feelings who is not psychotic.
8. The homosexual, or the parents of a homosexual, who feel he is an outcast.
9. The hospitalized parent worried about his or her children.
10. The discharged hospital patient emotionally insecure, and uncertain or dubious about his convalescence and full recovery.

(1) **The depressed patient who has a strong religious inclination.** The active church member draws comfort from his religious faith and depends upon it. When he becomes emotionally ill, he will gain comfort from his pastor's presence, just as he would if he were physically ill. These patients will desire prayer. The pastoral prayer should convey hope and reassurance with an unmistakable emphasis upon the love of God and the acceptance of God.

An aged Presbyterian physician came to our hospital as a patient. He had served as an official board member of his local church for many years. After he expressed the desire to see a pastor, his psychiatrist requested that I see him. He then spoke of his failure in life and the misery he suffered in the thought of God's disappointment in him. The story was related in a calm and studied manner. I accepted it as the searching of a sick mind, but suspected that just the opposite was true. This was later confirmed when I learned that he was an excellent doctor who had served his community well. Toward the end of my visit, he asked if we could have prayer together. I rose, closed the door and turned to him as he fell upon his knees beside his bed. I knelt beside him and prayed a prayer of reassurance and encouragement. When he rose he thanked me. . . . He was still sick; he still required shock treatment, but both his doctor and I felt that this call and those that followed helped to steady him. Upon his recovery, he wrote me a note of appreciation. Remember, the depressed person gets well if he can be prevented from committing suicide. Good pastoral care helps, as does good nursing care, good occupational therapy, good dietary, in addition to good psychiatric care.

(2) **The grief suffering person.** A college professor developed

feelings of anxiety following the death of his mother. These feelings developed several months later. They were further complicated by a serious automobile accident in which the wife of a close friend was seriously injured, while he was driving. The professor became so anxious that he was unable to attend to the duties of his office and had to have psychiatric help. In addition to psychiatric interviews he was encouraged to talk with his pastor about his feelings toward his mother. These conversations, held once a week for six weeks, led to the expression of grief feelings that previously had been suppressed. The professor's grief feelings involved a dependency toward his mother from an earlier part of the man's life that had never been explored. The pastor's symbolic role and the mother's own life of religious faith set the stage whereby the son could speak with ease to the minister about these problems, and find relief. The psychiatrist dealt with other feelings, particularly those that had to do with the injury of his friend's wife, which in turn rested upon earlier problems.

(3) **The person suffering guilt which comes as the result of marital difficulty** often goes to a psychiatrist because there have been so few professional persons with whom these people could talk. The pastor who knows what he is doing can be of significant help. Unfortunately, he is typed by most people as a moralist. Whenever he shows acceptance and understanding toward a person in marital trouble, his helping role can often be more meaningful than that of the psychiatrist who is typed as having no opinion upon moral problems. The psychiatrist, recognizing this situation, may inquire of a patient if he has talked with his pastor.

(4) **The person who has broken the law and feels guilty about it.** Here the pastor may play a significant role. An elderly man killed his wife. He did not intend to kill her or even to hurt her, but he just "beat her too long," as he said. She had nagged at him for years. One day, in a fit of temper, he began to beat her with his cane. When he recovered his senses she was dead. In the psychiatric examination, which judged him to be sane, the man expressed regret for his action. The psychiatrist inquired about his church affiliation and learned that although he had been inactive for many years, he retained membership. The pastor was called and was able to be of considerable comfort to the man. A similar experience came to my

attention several years ago when a doctor had been arrested for selling drugs. In neither case was the patient psychotic. Both instances revealed guilt feelings of a conscious nature and a sense of isolation. We would maintain that these are problems with which religion has traditionally dealt and with which it should continue to deal.

(5) **The person under psychiatric treatment who wonders if his religious faith is valid, since he needs psychiatric treatment.** A minister who had been referred to a psychiatrist by his physician came to see me. I asked, "How can I help you?" He replied sheepishly, "I guess it's because these psychiatric interviews are painful." I asked, "Are they productive?" He responded enthusiastically, "They will probably turn out to be the most important thing that has happened to me during my whole education."

"Then why are you in here talking to me?" I asked, seeking to get the responsibility back upon his shoulders and yet not appear to be rejecting.

"Because I feel guilty in not being able to solve my problem myself through my faith."

I thought about that and then inquired, "Have you, as a minister, ever told people that their problems could be solved through their religious faith?"

He replied, "Many times."

"Do you feel now that people with religious faith have problems?" I asked.

He hesitated.

"Do you feel that Jesus had problems?" I added.

He smiled, getting the point, then added, "I see you are not going to pull my feet away from the fire. I guess I didn't really want you to, but I needed some encouragement." His later interviews with the psychiatrist went better, he later reported, because he settled down to facing the real issues involved in his emotional crisis.

(6) **Many people who have tried to commit suicide and failed feel guilty about what they have done.** Although they are no longer suicidal, they believe they have committed a serious sin. Of these, some feel they cannot be forgiven. A conversation with an understanding pastor will do much to reassure them. In fact, a pastoral conversation is almost routinely indicated, especially in those instances where the person has previously had a church or religious

affiliation. The pastor who views the attempt at suicide as the act of a person sick of mind can be of considerable assistance in helping him to re-establish his lost sense of dignity and the meaningfulness of life.

(7) **Many people disturbed by crises, but not psychotic, are under the care of a psychiatrist who may request that a pastor see the patient.** A woman, following the birth of a child with a birthmark upon its face, became quite depressed, asking, "Why has God done this to my baby? Why is God punishing my baby when it should be me?" At the request of the attending psychiatrist, her pastor came to see the woman. During his third call, when the pastor inquired as to why she felt God was punishing her child, she told of a love affair during the war while her husband was away from home. The birthmark upon her child's face was God's punishment, she thought. The pastor listened to her confession and reassured her concerning God's love and forgiveness. After talking with the doctor, the pastor was sufficiently informed to give her further reassurance about plastic surgery for the child which would remove the birthmark. Thus, the pastor was able to combine practical reassurance on a surgical topic with that which was peculiar to his role as a pastor.

(8) **While the homosexual or his parents consult the psychiatrist, they also need pastoral help.** Such persons may receive a great deal of comfort from talking with a wise and understanding pastor. Many pastors will be censorious in counseling the homosexual; others will not. Censorship and moralization will not be helpful. A mother and father consulted me about their twenty-six-year-old son living with a male companion. He had told his family that he had every intention of continuing the relationship. The parents questioned what they should do. I inquired as to their thoughts on the matter. They had no strategy except to break off all relationships with their son. This would clearly demonstrate their sharp disapproval of his behavior. "What would that accomplish," I asked, "except to isolate you from a son whom you love and who needs your love as you need his?" "We do not want to break with him," they reported. "Why should you, then?" I asked. "Just whom are you impressing; yourselves, your friends, God?" They were uncertain.

I then inquired if they had any clues as to why their son should prefer male to female companionship. They admitted they knew practically nothing. From my attitude of acceptance and encouragement, they seemed to draw comfort, and I was able to convey to them my own attitude of neither approving nor disapproving the boy's action.

Further inquiry was made concerning the constructive nature of the relationship between the son and his friend. That is, does this friendship contribute in a positive way to the life of the son? Is he happier, is his work better, is he a more useful and energetic person? Is this better than having him carry on a promiscuous relationship with whomever he might pick up? This is not to approve nor disapprove of his behavior, for such attitudes would have contributed nothing. What I was seeking to do was to help a mother and father accept a situation which was beyond their control.

(9) **The hospitalized parent who is worried about his or her children** will often receive a great deal of reassurance from a pastor. A woman patient in a state mental hospital was asked by her pastor whether anyone had been helpful to her while she was there. She replied, "That Lutheran pastor (chaplain of the hospital) who came to my room and sat down and let me talk about my children." While the psychiatrist, or the nurses, or the social worker, may have let her talk about her children, the pastor was a person in a role that was more familiar to her. She had a pastor back home who had talked with her about her children, and here he was again—a different man, of course, but still a pastor. Rapport was readily established on this basis.

(10) **The discharged hospital patient needs someone with whom he can talk regularly.** He needs to express his feelings to someone from whom he can draw encouragement and emotional support; someone who can evaluate his behavior sufficiently to know whether he is losing ground. The pastor may, in fact, be virtually the only person in many a community who knows the most elemental facts about mental illness and the art of listening. Such pastors should be briefed by the psychiatrist or medical social worker and be given the assurance that they have an open line of communication with the hospital whenever such professional help is needed.

A pastor told me of a visit he made to a woman recently released from a state hospital. He saw her once each week, but was unable to establish a good relationship with her. She continued to be shy and withdrawn. The family reported her to be difficult and felt that she was not trying to adjust to life at home. Yet, they had not reported her behavior to the hospital lest the authorities request her readmission. A few weeks later she ran away from home and was not found for several months. The pastor had not been contacted by the psychiatrist or social worker, and he did not feel enough confidence in his observations to call the hospital himself or to urge the family to call.

Miss P., a forty-year-old, unmarried schoolteacher, lived with her married sister following her discharge from the state mental hospital. The pastor called upon Miss P. regularly and studied her conversation. He was dissatisfied with the progress she was making. He observed her mood and noted her references of self-depreciation. He discussed these things with Miss P.'s sister and was told that the family did not know what to do with her. She did not fit into the family and seemed to make little effort to help herself. The pastor continued to call and noted that Miss P.'s condition seemed to be getting worse, but he still took no action either to consult with the family physician or to call the state hospital psychiatrist or chaplain. (We suggest calling the chaplain because he is usually more readily contacted than the psychiatrist. In a private hospital the psychiatrist would always be called.) A few weeks later, Miss P. committed suicide. Such a tragedy could have been avoided, if the pastor had been alert and knowledgeable about procedure.

It is a relatively simple matter for a local pastor to arrange to see a person who needs additional encouragement once a week for the first few weeks following his or her return from a hospital. Counseling sessions at such a time may make the difference between additional improvement and some serious relapse. At such a time, the pastor does not serve as a therapist but as a trusted friend who listens and is interested. Anxieties, frustrations, irritations, hostilities, hopes, and ambitions are freely discussed with the pastor who is available following the patient's return home. Some may ask, how does this differ from the psychiatrist's function? It may not be essentially different. But, the line of demarcation need not concern us. The pastor has always functioned in his own role as shepherd and he should not default in this phase of his ministry.

If the parishioner shows signs of relapse, fails to keep appointments and seems to be losing ground, the pastor should—after consultation with responsible members of the family—inform the psychiatrist of the patient's condition and seek his advice. Frequently, the psychiatrist is so busy that the minister will hesitate to make a formal appointment to discuss a parishioner's mental state. An easy method of communication is a short note to the physician. This is a proper and acceptable procedure where the minister is aware of difficulties that he suspects the doctor does not know.

Psychiatrists in state and V.A. hospitals are generally carrying case loads far in excess of accepted standards. The obvious consequence is that even with the use of social workers there is often inadequate follow-through at the local level where community resources are involved. Furthermore, the active and informed interest of pastors in the mentally ill is so recent that psychiatrists and social workers seldom think of the pastor as a local resource for contact and referral.

Most state and all Veterans Administration hospitals now have chaplains. The pastor who has a parishioner admitted to a V.A. or state hospital may communicate with the chaplain concerning his calling upon a patient. It is a simple matter for the chaplain to reach the psychiatrist in charge of the patient's section and discuss with him the patient's condition and the advisability of a call on a patient by his pastor. The chaplain can then communicate with the pastor, informing him when he may call. The institutional chaplain will usually offer to accompany the pastor to meet the patient, directing him through multiple corridors and opening numerous locked doors. This is a simple matter for the chaplain who walks the wards daily and who is known to the staff. For the average minister, paying his first visit to this hospital for the mentally ill, a state or V.A. hospital is a formidable experience.

Thus, the patient becomes acquainted with the chaplain in a personal way, identifying him with his own pastor and the church back home. When the patient is ready for discharge, the pastor is known to be interested and may be called upon to serve in a supportive relationship during the early days after his discharge when he feels particularly shaky.

While great gains have been made in cooperation between psychiatrists and pastors, far greater gains arc expected in the future. The minister, in referring a person for psychiatric care, should work closely with the family physician as the general practitioner will not appreciate the minister making such a referral without his knowledge.

Psychiatrists are always talking about the minister not getting in "over his depth" in counseling. Obviously, the psychotically ill person should be referred for treatment. Beyond this "the depth" of the pastor is limited only by his training and his time.

APPENDIX A

The GROWING EDGE of PASTORAL CARE

Opportunities

1. **The Military Chaplaincy.** There is a steadily growing recognition that counseling is an important part of the military chaplain's responsibility throughout the services. In many posts the chaplains serve not only the serviceman but his family as well. A limited number of chaplains are able to secure advanced study in counseling through special assignment while in the service.

2. **Veteran's Administration Hospitals.** The establishing of the Veteran's Administration Hospital Chaplaincy service was one of the important steps forward in pastoral care at the close of World War II. This work is now accepted as an important part of the care of the patients throughout the V.A. Hospitals. The chaplain must be a veteran. For information write to Veteran's Administration Hospital Chaplaincy Department, Washington 12, D.C.

3. **General Hospital Chaplaincy.** This opportunity is steadily expanding, although it still has a long way to go. Many non-sectarian general hospitals still have not recognized the importance of a clergyman or clergymen as integral parts of the staff. Also, many chaplains still work independently of the physician and the physician works independently of the chaplain. In time this gap will be closed. Specialized training beyond the B.D. degree is essential for the clergyman serving this position. For information write Director, Chaplaincy Service, American Protestant Hospital Association, 840 N. Lake Shore Drive, Room 640, Chicago 11, Ill.

4. **Mental Hospital Chaplaincy.** Chaplains are now employed in practically all state hospitals as well as in hospitals under the direc-

tion of the United States Board of Public Health. Work in private mental hospitals is still limited. Extensive specialized training beyond the B.D. degree is required. General opinion is that two years supervised study is desirable. For information write to the Chaplain of any state mental hospital. Failing this, write to Chaplaincy Department, St. Elizabeth's Hospital, Washington 20, D.C.

5. **Prisons and Correctional Institutions.** Chaplaincy service is well established in federal and state prisons. It is growing in reformatories and correctional institutions for youngsters. Specialized training is required for these positions. For information write Department of Pastoral Services, National Council of Churches, 475 Riverside Drive, New York 27, New York.

6. **Homes for Older People.** Chaplaincy services vary in these homes. All too often the chaplain's work is limited to conducting Sunday services of worship and to public relations. Counseling is essential in such homes. At present there is no organization of Chaplains serving such homes and no central office where one can write for information.

7. **Industrial Chaplaincy.** This opportunity is still largely unexplored although significant work has been done in some industries. Outstanding in our experience is that at Reynolds Tobacco Company, Winston-Salem, North Carolina. By and large industry has not accepted responsibility for providing pastoral counseling for its people, although the claim is frequently made that its employees are the most valuable asset an industry has. If this be true, well-trained counseling chaplains have a contribution of importance to make in industry. My own experience of working in industry, at the Myrtle Desk Company, High Point, North Carolina, in 1959, supports this belief.

8. **The Counseling Center.** The counseling center, such as I direct in Orlando, Florida, and R. Lofton Hudson directs in Kansas City, is still in the experimental stage. In both instances the community response indicates the willingness of people to seek and pay for counseling carried on by clergymen. The preparation for this task should be the most extensive of all for here the counselor is strictly on his own. I would feel at least two years of supervised

clinical study and at least five years experience beyond the formal study is desirable as preparation for work in a counseling center. There is no organization of pastoral counselors serving such positions.

9. **Pastor of Counseling in the Large Church.** Some large churches are now employing pastors with specialized training in counseling as members of their staff. This is still in a state of experimentation as said in Chapter 6. Another plan is for two or more churches in a community to employ a counselor. This is desirable in my opinion over the single large church as an office can then be established in a neutral situation. Such a plan is being followed in Nashville, Tennessee.

10. **Teaching Pastoral Care in the Theological Seminary.** Most of the major seminaries now have departments of pastoral care with one or more instructors. While the content of the instruction varies from one seminary to another, there is general agreement that such instructors should have specialized study in the field of clinical pastoral education and preferably should have carried major responsibility in a clinical program. An advanced degree beyond the B.D. is required. A few academic institutions now give such degrees in pastoral care. Write to Boston University School of Theology, 745 Commonwealth Avenue, Boston 15, Massachusetts; Garrett Theological Seminary, 2121 Sheridan Road, Evanston, Illinois; Southern Baptist Theological Seminary, 2825 Lexington Road, Louisville 6, Kentucky.

11. **The Local Church.** The opportunity for counseling in the average local church is limited only by the pastor's training, time and energy. Serious mistakes have been made by pastors with special training in counseling giving an undue amount of time to non-parishioners who need help and neglecting their own parishioners and church work. The pastor of the local church should avoid becoming a specialist in any phase of pastoral care. He is a general practitioner.

Preparation

Most of the major theological seminaries now have instructors of pastoral care who have had advanced study in clinical pastoral education. In the introductory courses in pastoral care in the theological seminary the student for the ministry receives his introduction to clinical study for, even though opportunity for clinical pastoral experience may not be an integral part of these courses, all instructors use clinical material in their presentations. Extensive opportunities are now available in almost all sections of the country for summer study, and more are being made available all of the time. These courses range from five to six weeks to twelve weeks in length and are conducted in mental and general hospitals and in prisons and reformatories. Advanced study of from six months to two years is available in several places, some of which offer degrees; others do not, but give excellent supervised training. The advanced academic degree is a union trade card which is required by most theological seminaries.

As the leaders in the field of pastoral care get older we seem to feel our younger colleagues need more and more study to be counselors. They actually do for the field advances so rapidly, but we are creating something of the same problems the specialty boards in medicine have created. We must be careful not to try to legislate who shall and who shall not help people in trouble. While a pastor or physician needs all the study and training he can acquire, study alone will not make him a good counselor.

Each January the magazine, *Pastoral Psychology,* Manhassett, New York, publishes a list of institutions with brief descriptions where study and training in clinical pastoral education may be obtained. To counsel without training is like preaching without instruction; one may pull it off once in a while but as a steady diet it gets pretty thin and, what is even more serious, it is certain to do untold damage. Every time a person seeks counseling and does not receive it, it makes it more difficult for the next counselor or therapist who seeks to help that person.

APPENDIX B

SIXTEEN TIMES

to SEND

for a PASTOR

1. When a loved one is seriously ill and facing death.
2. When a relative continues to be despondent following the death of a loved one.
3. When you are facing a surgical operation.
4. When you are facing adjustment to a physical handicap.
5. When you are going through a long convalescence.
6. Following the birth of a baby.
7. When you desire to join the church.
8. When you have begun to worry about excessive drinking.
9. When a loved one is drinking excessively.
10. When you are having difficulty in your marriage.
11. When you are choosing a life work and feel uncertain about your choice.
12. When you are choosing a life mate and have doubts about your choice.
13. When as a parent you are concerned about either of the above for your son or daughter.
14. When you are discouraged and life has lost its meaning.
15. When a loved one has become despondent for no obvious reason.
16. When the behavior of a loved one shows marked and rapid change, whether it is toward excessive misbehavior or excessive interest in religion.

BIBLIOGRAPHY

BOISEN, ANTON T., *The Exploration of the Inner World.* New York: Willett, Clark and Company, 1936. 392 pp.

———. *Out of the Depths.* New York: Harper & Row, Publishers, 1960. 216 pp.

CABOT, R. C. and DICKS, R. L., *The Art of Ministering to the Sick.* New York: The Macmillan Company, 1936. 384 pp.

CANNON, WALTER B., *The Wisdom of the Body.* New York: W. W. Norton and Company, 1932. 333 pp.

CRYER, N. S., JR., and VEYHINGER, J. M., *Casebook in Pastoral Counseling.* New York: Abingdon, 1962. 320 pp.

DICKS, R. L., *How to Make Pastoral Calls for Ministers and Laymen.* St. Louis: The Bethany Press, 1962. 64 pp.

———. *Meet Joe Ross.* New York: Abingdon Press, 1957. 159 pp.

———. *Pastoral Work and Personal Counseling.* Revised Edition. New York: The Macmillan Company, 1949. 195 pp.

———. *Toward Health and Wholeness.* New York: The Macmillan Company, 1960. 158 pp.

DUNBAR, FLANDERS, *Mind and Body: Psychosomatic Medicine.* New York: Random House, 1947. 263 pp.

HILTNER, SEWARD, *Pastoral Counseling.* New York: Abingdon Press, 1949. 291 pp.

KEMP, CHARLES F., *Physicians of the Soul.* New York: The Macmillan Company, 1947. 314 pp.

MCNEILL, JOHN T., *A History of the Cure of Souls.* New York: Harper & Row, Publishers, 1951. 371 pp.

MENNINGER, KARL A., *The Human Mind.* Third Edition. New York: Alfred A. Knopf Publishers, 1948. 517 pp.

OATES, WAYNE E., *The Christian Pastor.* Philadelphia: The Westminster Press, 1946. 171 pp.

———. *Anxiety in Christian Experience.* Philadelphia: The Westminster Press, 1955. 156 pp.

———, Editor, *An Introduction to Pastoral Counseling*. Nashville: Broadman Press, 1959. 331 pp.

ROGERS, CARL L., *Counseling and Psychotherapy*. Boston: Houghton Mifflin Company, 1942. 320 pp.

SCHERZER, CARL J., *The Church and Healing*. Philadelphia: The Westminster Press, 1950. 185 pp.

WISE, CARROLL A., *Pastoral Counseling, Its Theory and Practice*. New York: Harper & Row, Publishers, 1942. 279 pp.

INDEX